Americans in Australia

Americans in Australia

Ray Aitchison

CHARLES SCRIBNER'S SONS   NEW YORK

Printed in the United States of America
Library of Congress Catalog Card Number 72-11146
SBN 684-13264-8 (cloth)

Contents

Introduction   vii

1   The early Americans   1

2   Americans at the Eureka Stockade   25

3   Americans and Canberra   36

4   A land of mourning   46

5   The 1930s   50

6   The Yanks saved Australia   55

7   Post-War: The lost opportunities   76

8   The Vietnam confidence trick   86

9   The Hollywood pioneers   98

10   Americans in mining   114

11   Banana Republic   126

12   Institutional investment   138

13   The illusion of progress   152

14   Trade   166

15   The last option   178

16   Americanization   189

Bibliography   211

Acknowledgments

The material on George Francis Train (pp. 13-22) is taken from his letters, 1853-5, now republished by William Heinemann Australia under the title of A *Yankee Merchant in Goldrush Australia*, edited by E. Daniel and Annette Potts.

Introduction

This is the story of Americans in Australia and the American influence there. It is also the story of the last American frontier where many of the warm aspirations and ideals of an earlier United States still survive, unspoiled by the sourness of disillusionment.

It is unfortunate that most Americans know absolutely nothing about their own nation's vital involvement in the history and modern development of Australia. Significant events and people forming a continuous interchange between the two countries since the earliest days of Australian settlement have been neglected. In Australia, too, the teaching of history has consistently played down the American story.

Americans who go to Australia to find a land of fewer people, wide open spaces, more sunshine and clean air are not disappointed. Australia is an island continent of three million square miles, almost the same size as the United States but with a population of only just on thirteen million people. It remains a pioneering country with vast potential and increasing opportunities.

Paradoxically, Australians are the most urbanized people in the world. In 1972 their cities housed 88 per cent of the total population. The Australian cities are monuments to a chronic absence of real leadership. Most of the nation's wealth is being spent in five cities while the remainder of the continent is gently falling into the hands of foreigners, particularly Americans.

Australians often complain when they hear about the pioneering work that Americans are doing in the outback rural areas of their country, and they fix their antipathy onto U.S. ownership and profit-taking. But the Australians have been losing the guts and gumption to engage in pioneering themselves and to risk capital in the outback, and therefore have little right to complain. Their city dwelling has been narrowing their outlook and has been sapping their initiative and energies. If the American vigour and enterprise in Australia eventually arouse them from their inertia it will not be the first time that this has happened.

Inevitably some of the Americans who have emigrated to Australia have been exploiters and despoilers. This book will examine in some detail powerful U.S. financial operations in Australia, and the disadvantages as well as the contributions to the nation of U.S. money investment in Australia. It is strange but true that most Australians are still ignorant of the enormous extent of American ownership of their country.

Americans like the place. A philosopher from the United States, Professor Sidney Hook, declared in Sydney that he had found a culture and a way of life in Australia that he was as much prepared to defend as his own. He had found the same basic democratic habits and ideals that characterize the American political experience, only more leisurely and relaxed. Professor Hook felt so integrated in Australia that he was searching around for likely places where he might retire.

U.S. airlines advertise Australia as a frontier country, and this appeals greatly to American tourists. When they arrive the tourists find that Australian cities are so congenial and comfortable and conducive to the way of life they know and enjoy that few of them are keen to go out into the Australian bush and see the frontier. They are content to settle for cosy little demonstrations of 'Australiana' arranged by their travel agents close to town. After having seen a kangaroo in captivity or some gum trees and wattle in the suburbs they return to their American-style hotel to rest up for their next adventure.

At the U.S. base at Exmouth in rugged Western Australia I met a U.S. Navy officer who intended buying a pub in an Australian city when he had obtained his discharge from the Navy. American cotton farmers in northern New South Wales, U.S. businessmen in South Australia, and Texas cattlemen in the Northern Territory have come to think of Australia as God's own country.

All sorts of Americans have chosen Australia for a better way of life and for various reasons. They have included a lieutenant of the 28th Ladder Company of the New York Fire Department, John McDonald, who told everyone quite frankly that he thought Australia was the one place in the world where he could live well on his paltry pension.

A retired American petroleum engineer, Robert Wilhelm, formerly of San Diego, has found a more satisfying life for himself near Murwillumbah in New South Wales, raising donkeys.

The spirit and experience of American migrants is often to Australia's benefit. Usually they are not the kind of people who mutely and meekly accept authoritarian decisions that seem likely to lower the standard of the new life which they hope to build for themselves in Australia. They angrily oppose so-called progress if it will cause serious damage to the environment. U.S. migrants have seen the disastrous consequences of unbridled commercialism in their country, and frequently speak out against any repetition of American blunders in Australia. The experience of their homeland has made them much wiser than Australians.

I take heart from the fight put up by some Californian migrants in Queensland to prevent the mining of one of Australia's most beautiful beaches. The Californians had settled at Sunshine Beach, 90 miles north of Brisbane – a location as lovely as was the Californian coast fifty years ago. It was exactly what they had crossed the Pacific Ocean to refind. But in October 1971 along came a mining company with plans for dredging the beach to extract rutile from its sands. One of the Californians, Mrs Florence Peterson, deplored the apathy of Australians who stood by limply and dumbly and permitted bureaucrats and commercial interests to do what they wished. 'There's only one trouble with Aussies,' she said. 'As a whole they are extremely passive. Australians must be the most abused consumers in the world. They take everything on the nose.' Mrs Peterson took her fight against the sand mining company to the Mining Wardens Court. She was neither limp nor dumb. What she had said about Australians was right. The meek who inherit the Earth had better learn how to fight or someone not meek will surely take their inheritance away from them.

Australians give Americans a better reception than they receive almost anywhere else in the world. Australians do not regard American refugees as social dropouts who have fled the problems of their homeland. As long as Americans can stay out of trouble with the law in Australia, can support themselves and do not import America's national problems, they are most welcome to stay.

By necessity this book is almost entirely confined to the involvement of white Americans in the building of the Australian nation. American Negroes were to be found among the crews of U.S. sailing ships calling at Australian ports last century, and during the Second World War thousands of them were stationed in Australia with the U.S. armed forces, but because of Australia's long-established immigration restrictions few Negroes have lived there permanently.

It could almost be said that if Britain is the mother of modern Australia then the United States is the accidental father. Britain's submission to the United States in the American War of Independence brought about the conception of Australia. The British convicts who would have been shipped to America to become the foundation stock for future U.S. families were transported to Australia instead, and another New World country was born.

Until the Second World War Britain was overwhelmingly the dominating influence upon Australia but since

Britain began withdrawing into Europe the importance to Australia of British military protection and trade has declined greatly. Britain retains a substantial investment in Australia and still has the affections of Australians who come from British stock – but the United States is now leading fiddler Down Under and Australians have been dancing obediently to the American tune.

Australians used to believe that they were destined to become a great nation. It was not something they spoke about much but they had a quiet confidence in their future. Partly it was because they thought that they had sprung from greatness – Britain and the United States had stamped a family resemblance upon the face of Australia, and that encouraged hope. A more concrete reason for confidence came from possession of a continent that could provide Australians with all the natural resources they required. The United States and Russia had similar good fortune but few other countries.

However, the faith of Australians in their future has been waning. It has been undermined by doubts that they can retain their independence. A nation that dances to the American fiddle may be doing it from necessity, but does not enjoy it. And it is not a stepping-stone to greatness.

1

The early Americans

It began on a fine day when the smooth surface of Sydney Harbour was overlaid with the faint blue haze of early summer. Green and black cicadas were shrilling in the heavily timbered slopes around the foreshores, deafening in their appreciation of the increasing heat. Above the trees on the rocky northern shore were rising thin grey spirals of smoke from camp fires, and in the sheltered bays of the harbour natives were fishing from their bark canoes. On the nearby bare island of Pinchgut a white convict was staked out for punishment on the baking hot rock, groaning in his shackles.

The date was 1 November 1792.

The distant white speck on the horizon probably was seen first by the sharp-eyed blacks. It was the sails of a tall ship heading towards Port Jackson. One of Governor Phillip's sentries who had been instructed to keep watch for the expected arrival of a British supply ship fired a shot from his musket. Echoes rebounded from the sandstone cliffs and flocks of startled birds flew across the yellow beaches and over the thick forest nearby.

The American flag being run up to the mainmast startled the white inhabitants of Sydney almost as much as the musket shot had scared the birds. The news reached the chain gangs and a sudden light burned in the eyes of the convicts. Moments before they had been men without hope – outcasts in a settlement so remote from the rest of the world that only the British Navy which had put them there could find them again. Their settlement was on a lost continent on the other side of the world from Europe – yet here was a visiting ship and not from the British Navy.

The vessel was the *Philadelphia*. Her skipper, Captain Thomas Patrickson, was a seasoned Pacific Ocean mariner who had learned of the existence of the new convict settlement while on a recent voyage from the United States to China. For almost 150 years maps had depicted the Australian continent, except for the east coast. Ships' masters like Patrickson, who were scouts and conveyors for merchants, had not thought it worthwhile endangering their ships in unknown reef waters by visiting the place. But the foundation of the British penal colony in Australia had provided a new business interest. Captain Patrickson had thus become the first trader to call.

That night bonfires were lit on the harbour headlands, and an additional ration of rum was distributed among the privileged to celebrate a momentous event. At Government House Captain Patrickson handed to Governor Phillip a gilt-edged letter of recommendation which he had obtained from the British Minister to the United States, Mr Phineas Bond. Wise in the use of diplomacy in foreign ports, Patrickson had known that one required good references before attempting to conduct business with former enemies.

Phillip was pleased that the Americans had arrived. The colony had been running short on supplies. The *Philadelphia* had brought to Sydney a cargo of pitch and tar, some rum and gin, and some tobacco and beef. The cargo was a blessing in such a desperate place, but Patrickson made it known that if the British in Sydney would not buy it he could take his ship to China and sell it there. His hard-sell marked the beginning of a trading advantage which the United States has maintained against Australia to the present – even though U.S. relations with China are not quite what they were.

The *Philadelphia* was available to back-load to America, but Australia's export trade was not an easy starter. Nothing was immediately available to sell back to the U.S. Some good coking coal had been found near Sydney but no one had yet got around to mining it in commercial quantities. There was nothing else.

Governor Phillip remembered, however, the colony of convicts which he had placed on Norfolk Island, 800 miles out in the Pacific Ocean, to lessen the drain on resources available on the mainland of Australia. He asked Patrickson if he would take some supplies to Norfolk Island in the *Philadelphia* for a charter price. The American readily agreed.

As he sailed down Sydney Harbour on his way out, Captain Patrickson surveyed the beautiful shoreline with some regret. Only a few years earlier someone could have claimed the whole of Australia for the United States as Captain Cook had done arbitrarily for Britain ... but at least there remained a lot of cheap real estate available – as many other Americans were to discover during the next 200 years.

*

American ships soon began making the new port of Sydney a regular port of call. The next vessel after the *Philadelphia* was the *Hope* from Rhode Island, also with supplies for sale. She was well named. Every convict in Sydney looking at her hoped to smuggle himself aboard, with the assistance of the American seamen, and to escape into the outside world.

Some of the U.S. ships which put into Sydney Harbour were short of food and water, but for the first twenty years of the Sydney settlement its trade was almost exclusively with the United States. Australia did not begin to trade with Britain until 1807. Sixteen American ships called at Sydney up to 1800 and most of them were traders. Between 1800 and 1811 another thirty-five found their way there. Then followed a break of a few years due to war between England and America, but after the war American ships resumed visits to Sydney in steadily increasing numbers.

So valuable was the contribution to the Australian economy by American shipping that United States ships of all kinds were given equal rights with British ships in Australian ports – a most unusual concession in a

British colony. By the beginning of the nineteenth century so many American ships were carrying away escaped convicts from Sydney that the colonial authorities segregated all visiting American ships to a closely patrolled bay in the harbour, still known as Neutral Bay. American sea captains had to lodge a bond of £200 to be forfeited if convicts were found in their ships before leaving Sydney. This proved to be an ineffective deterrent. The bond was raised to £500, a large sum for those times. Australian friendship towards Americans truly began with those escape ships in Neutral Bay.

The Americans were envied by the Australians of the nineteenth century. They were a New World people who had broken free from Britain. The great American ideals of liberty, equality and independence were the dream of the harshly ruled and lonely Australians. For them it was an unobtainable dream unless one could escape to America.

Contrary to modern and popular belief a majority of the convicts of early Sydney were treacherous scoundrels, degraded and brutalized. Two-thirds of them had been professional criminals before having been sentenced in Britain to transportation. Many of the women convicts were prostitutes and women of violence. It was true, however, that some convicts were worthy of the Americans' sympathy and help. They had been exiled for trifling offences. Francis Flexmore, for example, had stolen two pairs of plated shoe buckles in London while drunk, and for that misdemeanour a magistrate had sentenced him to seven years transportation to the Australian penal colony. It was virtually a life sentence. No provision had been made to return any of the prisoners to their homeland after the completion of their terms of imprisonment, and it was highly unlikely that people like Flexmore would ever be able to save enough money in Sydney to pay their return fare.

Others among the convicts who were sure to arouse the Americans' sympathy were the Irish political prisoners. They had been sent to the southern hemisphere because they were incorrigible rebels always plotting for the over-throw of British rule. In Australia they had become the ringleaders in unrest and mutiny. So truculent and troublesome were some that their escape would have been welcomed by their overseers.

Reasons for the prevailing mood of rebellion and sullen hatred of authority in Sydney were plainly evident. The British, a nation of slavers who had made large profits transporting Africans to sweat in America, were now surpassing themselves by making slaves of their own kind in Australia. Labour on public works was being done to the accompaniment of the clanking of chains. The daily music of Australia's infancy was not the hymn-singing of pious pilgrims giving praise to God for having delivered them to a promised land. It was the chilling whistle of the punishment whip as it thudded into the cut and bleeding flesh of convict backs.

The American crews were hard cases themselves and not easily shocked, but some of the penalties meted out in the prison colony left them in no doubt as to whose side they were on. Two hundred lashes across the bared back was routine for stealing or for insubordination, and sometimes women convicts were flogged. By a miracle of endurance some men survived the extreme penalty of one thousand lashes. It left them crippled physically and spiritually, hunched over with stiffened backs and dead eyes, and they became walking medical curiosities. The occasional hangings in public seemed almost humane by comparison.

It has been calculated that in 1972 one in every fifteen Australians was descended from a convict. But then again many other Australians are the descendants of the roister-ing American seamen, adventurers and miners who were in their country. Naturally enough most modern Aus-tralians prefer to be reminded of early American ancestors than of early British or Irish convict forebears.

Much of the heavy despondency of the penal settle-ment was lifted when American sealers and whalers began using Sydney Harbour as a base for their operations in the

South Pacific. The crews of these ships were always ready for high spirited celebrations ashore after their arduous months at sea, and the locals were eager to help them spend their money. Prostitution enjoyed a bull market in Sydney every time the American fleets returned to port. Convict women rejoiced that the profession in which they had become so well practised in Britain had become profitable again. Thieving also prospered again. Many an American seaman was robbed of even his clothing while ashore. Brawls between the Americans and local louts were common, particularly in the tough Rocks district on the western bank of Sydney Cove.

Governor King worried about the much more bloody fights between local and American sealers at the hunting grounds of Bass Strait. The Americans' main objective in Bass Strait seemed to be the extermination of all the seal herds as quickly as possible. In August 1804, Governor King denied the use of Sydney to the American sealers as a base, but this had little effect. By then so many of the Bass Strait seals had been killed off that the industry was finished. The Americans concentrated instead on rum-running. This much more profitable and easier business was conducted in collaboration with Sydney merchants.

In 1833, Australia's first export cargo was loaded into the American vessel, *Tybee*, and was sent to the United States. It included 4,800 cattle hides, and 1,000 kangaroo skins. In the same year an American firm, Kenworth and Company, became the first traders to open a branch office in Australia. This led to the appointment of Mr J. H. Williams as the first U.S. Consul in Sydney.

The *Black Warrior* brought flour from the U.S. in 1833 and back-loaded thirty-three bales of wool. It was the first Australian wool exported direct to America – but the trade did not last long. The American Government imposed high duties to kill it in its infancy. This marked the beginning of a long history of hard and often unfair trade practices used by the United States against Australia. For the next 138 years Australians were to

protest regularly about the American tariff barrier shut-
ting out Australian wool and other farm products from
the U.S. market, but Washington was destined to remain
deaf to most of them. By 1971 Australia was to have an
unfavourable trade exchange of $500 million with the
U.S. and was to be still trying without luck to sell its
wool to the Americans. The early trade pattern endured.
   In 1839 the first cargo of ice ever landed in Sydney
arrived in the *Tartar*. 400 tons of the ice had been loaded
into the ship in Boston, and 250 tons of it remained un-
melted when the *Tartar* reached Sydney after its long
voyage through the tropics. Thereafter all the ice used
in Australia until 1860 was imported from the United
States. It was ungallant to have a scotch on the rocks
without a kindly thought for Uncle Sam – even if he
would not buy Australian wool. Stoves and carriages and
sewing machines made in America became popular with
the Australian public. Lamps which lit bush shacks
during the black nights were burning American kerosene.
   The first sailing ship built exclusively for the Australian
trade was constructed by the merchants of Salem
in the United States in 1847. She was the *Australia* of 534
tons. The little freighter back-loaded Australian flour,
timber, and coal to the United States. Sometimes she
had to wait for moorings in Sydney Harbour because by
then an American whaling fleet using the harbour was
often crowding the foreshore anchorages with more than
forty vessels. Another forty whalers stationed in the South
Pacific were using Hobart in Tasmania for a base.
   American pioneers who became resident in Australia
were responsible for better roads, improved mail services,
and for the establishment of many new industries. During the American Civil War they started tobacco-growing
in Australia. Irrigation of fruit trees in northern Victoria
was based on a system which had been perfected in
California and served as a pilot scheme for the great
Murrumbidgee Irrigation Area of later years. By the
1860s a U.S. coach manufacturer, Mr F. B. Clapp, was
running Melbourne's bus services. Later, Americans

started mining at Broken Hill in New South Wales, leading to the foundation of Australian heavy industry.

One of the most outstanding of all of the American pioneers was James Rutherford, born in Erie, U.S.A. Rutherford made a fortune in freight and passenger transportation, but was a many-sided businessman, successful in all he undertook. He arrived in Australia in 1852, became a gold miner, a stockman and horse dealer, a stage coach driver, and then the owner of the Cobb and Co. stage coach company which extended its services from Victoria to New South Wales and Queensland. Rutherford became a large-scale cattle rancher in New South Wales. His company developed the timber trade between Western Australia and India, and constructed the railroad between Glen Innes and Tenterfield in New South Wales. He raised sheep on open range property in Queensland, and imported prize bloodstock to improve Australian cattle herds on a scientific breeding basis. Most important of all, James Rutherford was one of the fathers of the Australian steel industry. He founded and financed the Eskbank Iron Works at Lithgow, the forerunner of the BHP iron and steel complex, Australia's most powerful industrial giant of modern times. Rutherford was that rare combination of visionary and practical businessman. He died in Queensland in 1911 at the age of 84.

A list of other nineteenth century Americans who made a lasting impression by their achievements in Australia would be a long one. Among the more interesting was James Mario Matra who proposed that a colony of American loyalists be formed in Australia. Nothing came of his scheme, but today a suburb of Sydney bears his name. And there was George Washington Lambert who became one of Australia's early painters, and Dion Boucicault, the American actor and director who influenced early theatre in Australia, and yet another American actor, Joseph Jefferson. Herbert Hoover, later President of the United States, was a mining engineer in Australia from 1896 to 1898. He returned for a second term in the Australian mines from 1905 to 1907.

John Greeley Jenkins was an American politician who did well in Australia. He was born in Pennsylvania in 1851, arrived in Australia in 1878 as a book salesman and stood successfully for election to the South Australian parliament. He became Premier of South Australia at the turn of the century after having been Minister for Education and Commissioner of Public Works. Jenkins also had been Minister controlling the Northern Territory – a quarter of the total area of Australia, but inhabited at that time mainly by wild Aborigines. For Americans it was to become a second Texas.

Sydney Harbour where it all started has remained a favourite port of call for American ships – particularly for the United States Navy. The arrival of the 'Great White Fleet' in Sydney in 1908 was the event of a lifetime. The fleet consisted of 16 American battleships and 5 auxiliaries under the command of Rear Admiral Charles Sperry. In 1925 another American fleet of 10 battleships and 4 cruisers called and Australians travelled hundreds of miles to Sydney to see them. In more recent times so many American fleets have been in and out of Sydney that the port has become almost another San Diego.

The biggest surprise that the American Navy ever sprang on Sydney, however, occurred on the night of 29 November 1839. An American naval scientific expedition commanded by Commodore Charles Wilkes, entered the harbour unobserved after dark. At daybreak the following morning the citizenry awoke to find all of the Wilkes ships at anchor within easy bombardment range of their city. Had Wilkes commanded an enemy fleet he could have captured Sydney overnight with the utmost ease.

Even then the authorities in Australia were nervous that one day the Russians would come. They were shocked by the lesson and decided to build a fort in Sydney Harbour. They placed it on Pinchgut Island – a squat stone tower and barracks they called Fort Denison. It is a picturesque structure totally useless for defence but now much photographed by American tourists. The man who measures the rise and fall of tides in Sydney Harbour lives there. Until recently he fired a ceremonial cannon every day at noon.

Americans visiting Australia are likely to prefer Sydney to Melbourne. Usually they find that Sydney is more of a fun city, more of an informal international city. Melbourne is quieter. It is more conservative and businesslike. Melbourne plays Boston to Sydney's New York. Yet Melbourne has a rugged past and remains the centre of Australian nationalism.

More than one hundred years ago the city was the main supply and entertainment base for the new goldfields of Victoria and the temporary home for thousands of gold-rush miners from the American west coast. These Americans took with them to Melbourne a fervent belief in the need for every country to become a republic. They believed in the rights of the individual – each concerned mainly with his own rights – and they had an inclination towards riot and rebellion if they felt hampered by the power of established authority. Together with exiled Irishmen they were firebrands who put a fighting spirit into the place. They were loud dissenters and rowdy agitators who shoved the people of Australia towards the road to self-rule.

The gold discoveries of California and in eastern Australia in the 1850s were like an explosion, scattering the populations of both countries to either side of the Pacific Ocean. The gold rush in California created a keen demand for commodities from Australia to supply the rapidly enlarged population of western United States. Sydney merchants established trading branches in San Francisco. They exported beer, building materials, flour, timber and coal to California. These exports in 1850 were worth £95,473, and eighty-six ships were engaged in the trade. However, with the discovery of gold in Australia, exports to California declined and American exports to Australia correspondingly increased. It had been good for Australian businessmen while it had lasted. Since then the balance of trade with the United States has never been in Australia's favour.

When the news of the Australian gold strikes reached the United States an army of American miners deserted unprofitable claims on the Californian goldfields and took the first available ships westwards across the Pacific. Many of the vessels in which they travelled had been whaling or sealing ships which had been hastily converted to carry passengers. They did not carry them in comfort.

The heavy two-way traffic of miners inevitably caused trouble and ill-feeling between the two countries. Former convicts and other hard-bitten characters from Australia ran foul of the law in California, while Californian miners arriving in Australia were considered to be the scum of the North American continent, too ready to shoot first and argue later. In California the authorities introduced immigration restrictions to stop Australian undesirables from landing. When this became known in Australia there was immediate public indignation and resentment. The Melbourne newspaper, *The Argus*, led the attack with a stinging editorial advocating that similar immigration laws be introduced in Australia to keep out undesirable Californians.

Lord Robert Cecil, who was to become Marquis of Salisbury and three times Prime Minister of Great Britain, went to the Australian goldfields at the age of twenty-two and his diary includes a graphic description of a Californian gold prospector who travelled with him to the Victorian gold diggings in a spring cart:

'He was a coarse, hideous, dirty-looking man, without an attempt at ornament or even neatness in his dress; yet he wore in his ears a pair of earrings about the size and shape of a wedding ring. He wore a pair of pistols in his belt, and the words, "put a bullet through his brain" were continually in his mouth . . . .'

Before 1851 and the discovery of gold the population of Melbourne had been only 24,000. Two years later the population had grown to 200,000, and the goldrush had transformed Melbourne into a roaring boom town swept by clouds of dust in dry weather but deep in mud every time it rained. Its original buildings had become lost in the great surrounding encampment of tents and shacks. It had become a city of murder and robbery by night or by day, a city of tumult, danger and confusion, and a city with 100 brothels. Family men who had lately emigrated from Britain took one look at Melbourne and hurried their families back on board ship again. Women and children landed too soon in Melbourne by their impatient menfolk often had to sleep at night on bare ground because of a shortage of beds. A contemporary writer gave this eye-witness account of the scene at one of the city's banks: 'Miners in blue woollen frocks and corduroy, with a fagged and wretched appearance were getting their small bags of gold changed into cash. One fellow rubbed his face as we stood by and as he had been previously putting his hand into the gold dust one side of his face appeared perfectly gilt.' A report of a Melbourne wedding at that time stated that the bride was drunk and fraternizing with the populace and was seen leaning with bottle in hand from the carriage window.

There had long been a fear among the administrators of Australia that any discovery of gold would put the convict mobs beyond control. A clergyman who earlier had found some traces of gold had been warned to keep his discovery absolutely secret if he did not want all decent people in the country to have their throats cut. However, a striking resemblance between some parts of Australia and gold-bearing country in California had spurred on prospectors until major finds had been located. Some of the worst fears of the administrators were realized as the goldrush gathered pace. Freed convicts headed for the goldfields with former prison guards, American desperados and British deserters. Escaped convicts from Tasmania became bandits who killed without a qualm. Services broke down as storekeepers, clerks, bush workers, civil servants and ships' crews left their jobs and sought to get rich quickly, believing that gold nuggets could be picked up in handfuls.

An account of the first day of a rush at one of the Australian goldfields describes hundreds of desperate men all trying to defend as much ground as they could hold until Government surveyors arrived to peg out their claims to make them legal. Acres of ground covered by a seething carpet of humanity, men lying on their backs all over the paddocks throughout the day with legs and arms outstretched to cover as wide a section for their claim as possible, and all of them waiting for the surveyor. Many of the men were clutching a pistol in one hand and a knife in the other.

Part of the craziness of the goldrush sprang from the idea that it was a free handout from Nature and that anyone who could grab fast enough had the right to keep what he had seized. In Australia, where the tradition of trying to get something for nothing at every opportunity had already become well established, the goldrush craziness was chronic. Sometimes men went crawling into tunnels dug by other miners to grab gold as it was loosened from the soil. It is recorded that a Kentuckian found such a thief at the bottom of a shaft he had dug, scurrying around like a rat and so intent on picking up small nuggets and specks of gold that he was unresponsive to all warnings to stop. The Kentuckian applied the law of ownership by dropping a heavy piece of quartz eight feet down the shaft onto the man's head, laying him out cold. They dragged the unconscious thief to the surface, emptied his pockets and threw him into a creek.

Between August and December in 1851 more than 211,000 ounces of gold reached Melbourne from the new Victorian diggings. The fabulous Welcome Stranger nugget found at Ballarat in Victoria weighed 2,284 ounces. Houlterman's Nugget, uncovered later at Hill End in New South Wales weighed 7,560 ounces.

An American businessman, George Train, found the road to the Victorian mines strewn with broken carts, old drays, dead bullocks and horses in all stages of decay and 'everything that was sickening to the sight'. Bullock waggons were creaking and groaning along the rough tracks carrying freight at a price of £150 a ton. 'I suppose that in no place in the world is there such cruelty to animals as here', Train wrote. 'The poor bullocks in their iron bowed yokes being the great sufferers. The driver's whip is as long as a fishing pole and the crack of it as loud as a pistol shot.'

Throughout every night miners kept up a desultory fire with their weapons to warn ill-disposed persons that they were armed – and the danger of being hit by stray bullets was considerable. Train observed: 'The moment the sun goes down you have a perfect bedlam in the camp – screeching, swearing and singing, pistol shots and barking dogs all mingled together'. About 80,000 people were living in tents and shanties on the goldfields. Many of them regularly became high on 'New England champagne' – a potent aerated beverage introduced by American miners which sometimes exploded in the bottles like a bomb.

George Francis Train, merchant, traveller, historian and revolutionary-republican, arrived in Melbourne aged twenty-four in his company's ship, *Bavaria* on 21 May 1853, at the peak of the goldrush and at a time when merchants were making a pile of money there. Train had forced his way into the business firm of a relative, Colonel Enoch Train of Boston, and had been sent to Melbourne to establish a new branch of the company to be known as Caldwell, Train and Company.

Hundreds of ships were anchored in the port of Melbourne, most of them heavily laden with cargo and waiting to be unloaded. Train deplored the antiquated lighterage system and the fact that there were no wharves. He saw many opportunities in Melbourne as he walked around the raw city, impeccably dressed, carrying a cane and with a veil wrapped around his face to shut out some of the dust. Soon other American businessmen were telling him they were making profits of up to 200 per cent.

Train built a new office and warehouses with iron window shutters to keep out thieves, but he spent much of his time in the Criterion Hotel in Collins Street which had become a favourite meeting place for Yankees. The Criterion Hotel was a marvel for a frontier town. It had a grand and lofty Grecian hall of noble dimensions and most elegantly fitted out as a billiard saloon. It also possessed other refinements including an excellent barbers' shop, a bath house with hot or cold vapor or shower baths, a theatre to hold 500 people, and a bowling saloon. The dining room had a splendid reputation, and the hotel's cellars were stocked with fine wines. In the public bar the American barmen were as skilful as jugglers, pouring beer into glasses at great speed and whipping the glasses out along the bar to customers with a flourish and without spilling a drop.

The American proprietor of the Criterion Hotel, Sam Moss, was intent on introducing to Melbourne a style of quality and service not previously known there. All the people of prominence and power from the Governor down patronized the Criterion. In fact, some of the gentlemen of Melbourne were there sometimes before breakfast for 'phlegm-cutters'. The Criterion had a skylight through which was thrust a flagpole every 4 July, and up which was run the Stars and Stripes. The sign across the front entrance to the hotel proclaimed 'Ice, Ice, Ice'. But one of the main sights of the hotel was provided by its American customers – a striking lot with broad-brimmed hats and sashes around their waists, and bell-bottomed trousers. Their Uncle Sam beards wagged non-stop as they preached about profits and progress and American expansion – or spread-eagleism, as they called it.

In one of his letters home from Melbourne Train wrote 'You will be surprised to see how fast this place is becoming Americanized. Go where you will ... and you can but note some indication of the indomitable energy of our people ... The true American defies competition and laughs sneeringly at impossibilities. He don't believe in the word, and is prepared to show how meaningless it is.'

The American arrivals had brought with them to Australia new tools for mining. They had American axes and picks and shovels not available before in Australia. American merchants were importing alarm clocks and rocking chairs, iron stoves and bacon and flour. The first Boston water cart to lay the dust of Melbourne's streets was the start of the city's municipal services. It was a barrel-like arrangement which attracted great attention the first day it went to work. One man leapt up onto the cart to inform the driver that the thing was full of holes and was leaking. Shopkeepers who subscribed to the American watering service had the dust laid in the streets outside their premises several times each day, but those who did not contribute soon learned that the water cart could be turned off as it passed their door.

Americans established the Melbourne fire brigade on an efficient basis following a succession of disastrous blazes which had swept through the tent town to the newer more solid buildings. The Americans financed the brigade by raising (U.S.) $16,000 within a few hours one morning after such a fire. One hundred New York buggy waggons were imported, and soon these smart, light vehicles were the most desirable form of transportation in town. Americans won the contract to build the Hobson Bay Railroad Pier for Port Melbourne, and an American engineer, Sam McGowan, built the first telegraph line in Australia to flash news of approaching ships from the entrance of the port to the centre of the city. Other Americans were supplying Melbourne with fresh fish caught along the coast, and yet others were cutting firewood for the city on speculation and were making a good business of it.

Train established Melbourne's stock exchange in temporary premises, contributing the first membership fee of three guineas and encouraging other businessmen to do the same for the benefit of being able to meet and bargain, buy and sell. It was proposed that a statue of Queen Victoria be erected outside the stock exchange, but Train made the suggestion that a statue of George Washington should also be placed there because of the strong American influence in Melbourne.

By 1 January 1854 Train was depressed. He was thinking of his friends back home in Boston who were celebrating the new year in the white snows of mid-winter. He wrote 'Here I am sans icc, sans fruit, sans everything but the blues, the Australian indigo blues! Who can help it when suffocating with heat, eaten up with flies, and choking with dust. Twenty-five cents for a little dried up peach, $2 for a quart of cherries, 50 cents for a seed cucumber ... Give me the rainy season with all its mud and dampness rather than this pestilential fiery scorching dust-choking sirocco which almost drives me mad. The country far and wide is parched with the intense heat and the few cattle arc dying for food and water.'

By that time Train had come to realize that he was living in Britain's largest sullage pit, filled with the worst of humanity which had overflowed from Newgate and other prisons. He had fallen into the habit of glumly looking at the people he passed during his daily walks and wondering which was a burglar or a forger or a murderer. He recorded how two former convicts had recently been captured after having killed between fifteen to twenty people. During his first five months in Melbournc there had been eight or nine public hangings watched by thousands 'of the lower orders' of the population. They had included the execution of three of a gang of bandits who had ambushed a gold convoy and who had shot the escorting policemen off their horses. The following day Train was disgusted to see the blue-faced popeyed corpse of one of the hanged bandits on exhibition in the window of a drinking saloon. It had been decorated with flowers and ribbons. Nonetheless Train was confident that Melbourne would become a great city, although situated so far out of the way. He wrote: 'All we need is a little energy and a good deal of money to make the wheel turn rapidly. We must introduce a sprinkling of Yankeeism here and show the residents the meaning of despatch.'

Train conferred with another American, Freeman Cobb, of the American express agents, Adams and Company of Melbourne. As a result of this conference there was formed one of the greatest coach companies that the world ever saw – Cobb and Co., later owned by James Rutherford. The first four drivers of the Cobb and Co. stage coaches were Americans – John Peck, James Swanton, Antony Blake and John Lamber. They opened up with a fast parcel delivery and passenger service between Melbourne and the goldfields, driving recklessly at full gallop through the dust and ruts and heat in the best style of Wells Fargo and the Pony Express to get the mails through in quick time. Cobb and Co. became so successful that at the peak of its operations throughout eastern Australia it was harnessing 6,000 horses every day, and its coaches were travelling a total of 28,000 miles each week. Its coaches were Concords from the United States.

The drivers, like those driving similar coaches in the American West of the same period, had to run the risk of holdup men who wanted the mail and gold consignments they carried. Bushranger gangs frequently lay in wait outside towns, and it was a brave driver who tried to race his horses through their gunfire. Sometimes he became a dead driver. One holdup of a stage coach in south-eastern Australia was carried out by Frank Gardiner whose gang of seven included the infamous outlaw, handsome Ben Hall, and the Aboriginal renegade, Johnny Gilbert. The gang ambushed a Cobb and Co. coach and overturned it among boulders. They shot two of the police escort during the gunfight and got clear away with 2,715 ounces of gold, and a fortune in banknotes. Gardiner and his men did not wear fearsome body armour and helmets like the Ned Kelly of a later era. They moved fast and light, keeping one jump ahead of the pursuing police. They carried out other holdups around the goldfields until fate overtook them one by one. Some of them were caught and hanged. Police surrounded and shot down Johnny Gilbert and Ben Hall. At the mortuary they found that Ben Hall's body had fifteen bullets in it. Frank Gardiner was more fortunate. He was jailed, but was released and ordered out of Australia. He went to San Francisco where he became a saloon keeper. In 1903 Gardiner was shot during an argument in his saloon over a poker game and in the best outlaw style died with his boots on. His twin sons were alleged to have searched without success for the gold which the old outlaw was supposed to have buried near Mount Wheogo in New South Wales while he was on the run. But the story cannot be confirmed.

The constant flow of population between the United States and Australia during the period when Gardiner's gang was on the rampage, and while George Francis Train was making money more peacefully, caused an exchange of letters between uneasy British diplomats. It had become feared in London that dangerous ideas of freedom and equality among men, which had crossed the Atlantic from France to infect the United States, now were being carried across the Pacific to Australia.

On 30 August 1852, the British Consul in Philadelphia, Mr William Peters, had sent a confidential despatch to the British Foreign Secretary in London warning him that attempts to establish a republic in Australia were expected. The document was relayed from London to the Governor of Victoria to place him on his guard. 'Hundreds, if not thousands, of adventurers are either now on their voyage, or soon will embark from various parts of the United States for Australia – most of them bent "on extending the area of freedom" and on aiding their fellow men in the pursuit of Liberty and Republicanism. Indeed an Order, entitled the Order of the Lone Star, has been established here within the last twelve months and for this avowed purpose ... "to diffuse throughout the world the principles of Liberty and Republicanism ..."

'From the knowledge which a residence among them of twelve years has given me of the Americans, and especially of the class of them now on their way to Australia, I do not think that their presence will be attended by much good, and would have our authorities in that part of the world to be on their guard.'

The British Minister in Washington, Mr Crampton, on 31 October 1853, had sent yet another confidential despatch to London. 'There can be no doubt that a revolution in Australia by which its connections with Great Britain should be severed would be an event highly acceptable to the great mass of the American people.'

The ingredients for revolution always needed injustice and oppression to stir them and to make them react. Australia had those ingredients and in addition the dull resentment of authority in all its forms fed out from the convicts. There was also the festering anti-British hatred of the Irish exiles. The working class British migrants were still sore from the hardships and inequalities of the British industrial revolution and rigid class structure which they had hoped to leave behind them. People who had been born in Australia were impatient to be rid of their British governors and were being prompted by the American republicans in their midst to follow the example of the United States in breaking loose and standing alone.

Those apprehensive about the situation in Australia, however, did not understand that it was too early in that country for a full-scale and sustained uprising against British rule. Australia was a country of great distances between homesteads, settlements and towns and had few roads and slow communications. Injustice and oppression could not produce a universal reaction under those conditions. Furthermore there was a restless movement of population around the country in search of wealth which made people more willing to suffer oppression in any one district they happened to be in as being part of local hardships and only temporary until they could move elsewhere. Any revolutionary movement was destined to fail in Australia at that time because of the early stage of the country's development.

But there were many revolutionary triers. One was George Train who had written home on his first day in Australia that he had arrived in an embryo republic. Train rejoiced over the escape to America of an Irish political prisoner, John Mitchell, who had been on parole in Australia. He took a close interest in the colonial electoral system and was angered by its shortcomings. He ridiculed a move in Sydney by colonial autocrats for the establishment of a colonial peerage, and offered an alternative to all who would listen to him: 'Better a federal government à la America, the centre of which will be Melbourne.' He had been one of the Americans who had given a grand feast in the Criterion Hotel for 150 Irish spreaders of sedition, including that 'patriotic statesman, William Smith O'Brien and his companion in exile, Martin O'Dougherty'. Train had stated that the 'cankerous worm of English misrule' had been destroying their unhappy country when the Irishmen had thrown themselves into the excitement of the day.

Train became one of the first of a long line of people to make a political point out of the lack of defence in Australia. He pointed out that Australia was an easy mark for any country at war with Britain and that three decent sized warships could burn every port along the Australian coast. In the case of invasion months would pass before the Mother Country could give the least assistance. He deplored the fact that Australia had no flag of its own, and that most of the people in the colony had to pay taxes without being represented in the colonial parliament. Members of the Legislative Council of Victoria were elected for terms of ten years and had to be British born subjects aged at least thirty, and the owners of freehold property worth at least £10,000.

American merchants in Melbourne were unhappy about a tonnage duty of 24 cents a ton on all shipping, plus an import tax. But no tax in the colony was more unjust than that imposed by the colonial government upon the unfranchised miners on the goldfields. At a time when a labourer could earn only five shillings a day the miners were required to pay a licence fee of 710 shillings a year. Train was of the opinion that the miners were so numerous that they could successfully defy the Government. He wrote 'We possess every element of posterity – young in years, but old enough to slip the painter, cut adrift from the Old Country which hangs over us like an Incubus and become a nation of ourselves.'

American miners on the goldfields were soon becoming involved in daily disputes with police over licences. Governor Hotham, a thin-lipped former officer of the British Navy, had determined to increase revenue by a more thorough collection of licence fees. Against all advice he ordered that all licences be checked at least twice a week. More police were appointed to the goldfields, including former convicts from Tasmania, ex-prison warders and hoodlums. One of the police officers was Superintendent Armstrong who became known among the miners as the 'Flying Demon'. He carried a riding whip with a brass knob on the end of its handle as big as an apple, and which he often used to club down those who stood in his path. He chained one man to a tree for two days, although the captured miner was ill with bronchitis. The man died from exposure. The law enforcers on the goldfields included informers who kept half of the fines imposed upon the miners whom they betrayed to the police. Often the police took a percentage of the informers' cut. Therefore it happened that when Superintendent Armstrong was dismissed from his job in disgrace he left with the defiant comment that he had made £15,000 (sterling) in two years.

As the licence raids continued on the goldfields miners were harassed at their work, sometimes being required to climb out of deep mining shafts twice within an hour. Individual miners caught by the police in the open were beaten up and some were dragged off to prison in their saturated and muddy work clothes. Tentkeepers, cooks, shopkeepers and the servant of a priest were among those prosecuted for not owning miners' licences. Outraged Americans on the goldfields had formed a guerilla corps, partly out of bravado and partly out of defiance and a sense of national identification. Its original intention is now obscure. Possibly it could have had some connection with the American republican Order of the Lone Star – but it seems clear that its founders wanted to form the nucleus of a military organization which would go into battle when the time was right to challenge British authority. It was ironic that the avarice and unscrupulous methods of some of the American business community of Melbourne reduced the stiffening resolution of the American miners on the goldfields. The merchants had been importing guano from Peru but had not been able to obtain backloading for their vessels, and had been returning the ships unprofitably across the Pacific in ballast. They hit upon the criminal scheme of spreading false rumours that a new gold bonanza had been discovered in Peru to create a passenger traffic. Between January and March in 1854 twenty-two of the guano ships left Melbourne for Peru carrying American miners as back-loading. So awful were conditions in the overcrowded holds of the ships that an estimated 600 miners died on the voyages before reaching South America. Their bodies were thrown over the side to the sharks. However, Americans remaining on the Australian goldfields reformed their guerilla corps and called it the Independent Californian Rangers Revolver Brigade.

A unique representative of both the Irish and the Americans on the goldfields was a man known as Captain Brown. Brown, an Irishman, claimed to have been a Texas Ranger and to have lived with the Comanche Indians before travelling to Australia. He also had been a clerk for a slave auctioneer in New Orleans. Soon after his arrival on the goldfields in 1853 he called a meeting at Bendigo to complain that chaos would result if emigration to Australia continued at the present rate. Before long, however, he switched his attention to a more popular subject, the injustice of the high fees for miners' licences.

There was hostility towards Americans at Bendigo, especially after an American flag had been raised above a British flag in the presence of British miners. Nevertheless crowds of men gathered to listen to the Irish-American, Captain Brown when he railed against high licence fees. Together with a Mr G. E. Thomson and a Doctor Jones, Brown formed the Bendigo Anti-Gold Licence Association, and sent deputies to establish similar bodies on other goldfields. It was the beginning of organized resistance to the colonial government on the goldfields. The Bendigo Anti-Gold Licence Association obtained thousands of signatures on a petition forty feet long which was mounted on linen and tied with green silks. This petition demanded that the gold licence fee be reduced to 10 shillings a month. It was presented to Governor Hotham in Melbourne by Brown, Thomson and Doctor Jones. Later Brown was arrested and was removed from the goldfields. Other leaders took his place.

2
Americans at the Eureka Stockade

A sad disadvantage of life in a country which had started out as a penal settlement was the absence of anything in its short history of which its citizens could feel proud. Australia in the 1850s urgently needed heroes and the type of exploits which become food for national pride. Its working people, transplanted from other countries, needed a base upon which to build new traditions.

The British authorities also needed a sharp reminder that unless they took more care they would lose Australia in the same manner in which they had lost the United States. The battle of the Eureka Stockade at Ballarat on the goldfields of Victoria was the answer to all those requirements. Americans played a prominent part in providing it. They fought at the Australian version of the Alamo.

Karl Marx, who visited Australia in 1855, sought to make a socialist milestone out of the Eureka Stockade. He wrote 'It is not difficult to notice that these reasons (motives for the uprising) in reality are the same reasons which led to the declaration of independence of the United States of America, but with this difference – that in Australia the opposition against the monopolists, united with the colonial bureaucrats, arises from the workers.'

Mark Twain wrote about the stockade battle in his book *Following the Equator – A Journey Around the World*. He described the battle as the finest thing in Australian history and compared it with the conflicts of Concord and Lexington – all of them small beginnings but great in political results.

On 28 November 1854, the United States Consul in

Melbourne, Mr J. M. Tarleton, worried about the continuing trouble on the goldfields, attended a dinner at Ballarat. Most of the guests were Americans who were among some of the more responsible and respected of the U.S. miners. But also present was the Resident Commissioner of the goldfields, Mr Rede, whose autocratic intolerance had been causing much of the strife. Also there was the new police magistrate, Charles Hackett, an unloved dispenser of the law.

While the dinner was in progress the sound of shots was heard, and it soon became evident that Mr Tarleton's exercise in diplomacy was to be in vain. A military waggon coming into Ballarat had been attacked by miners. An American who had been driving the waggon under contract to the British Army had been injured and a drummer boy from the army escort had been accidentally trampled by the mob. The waggon had been overturned.

News of the attack was carried to the Americans' dinner and the messengers whispered urgently to Commissioner Rede and to Magistrate Hackett. Immediately afterwards Rede and Hackett excused themselves and hurriedly left the room. In loud voices the Americans began discussing the latest turn in events. Some of them wanted to leave and see for themselves what was happening outside, but the chairman at the dinner, Mr Otway, recalled them. Otway thought he saw his opportunity to achieve the Consul's purpose and disassociate all Americans on the goldfields from the mounting violence and disorder. Therefore he proposed a toast of considerable significance: 'Gentlemen, to Her Majesty, Queen Victoria.'

This was not well received. One of the American miners, Sam Irwin, expressed the feelings of himself and his friends by retorting 'While we must demonstrate loyalty of my fellow countrymen to the lawful ruler of their chosen country we will not pay our respects to her manservants, her oxen, or her asses ...' At that point Irwin indicated the newly vacated chairs of Commissioner Rede and Magistrate Hackett, and a burst of cheering resounded in the room. The U.S. Consul and Otway remained silent, frowning at their plates on the table before them.

The following day 12,000 miners assembled at Ballarat and afterwards flew their flag of independence. It was the Southern Cross, a flag with five white stars on a blue background, representing the conspicuous constellation peculiar to the night skies of the southern hemisphere. On instructions from the miners' leader, Irishman Peter Lalor, most of the men performed an act of treason by swearing allegiance to the new flag. Later it was claimed that a Declaration similar to the American Declaration of Independence had been prepared. A subsequent search for this document was unsuccessful.

Everyone on the goldfields knew that the police and the military would return in force. In fact reinforcements under the command of Major General Nickle with guns from two British warships had been ordered to Ballarat. The miners therefore constructed a stockade upon a low hill facing the military and police camp. 1,500 men, using thick slabs of mining timber and saplings, quickly put up a barrier of doubtful strength enclosing about one acre of land, and prepared to defend it.

One of the Americans who helped to build the stockade was a carpenter named Nelson, described afterwards as being a finely built man, full of energy and life. He was put in charge of the best group of defenders, but alas for Nelson. He had to contend with a complete absence of discipline among them. His men came and went as they pleased. They walked home to their tents or went off to work on their distant gold claims just as they felt inclined . . . and they were the best.

The rabble of miners within the stockade made some attempt to turn themselves into a fighting army within a few hours, and it would have been amusing had not the situation been doomed to tragedy. Bellicose Irishmen who did not have any firearms were dashing about with home-made pikes with which they were making practice thrusts and murderous flourishes like boys playing at war. The pikes were long poles with sharpened iron heads which had been manufactured for them by John Hafele, a German blacksmith from Wurtemburg.

The Independent Californian Rangers Revolver Brigade arrived at the stockade. This was the heroic scene for which the Californians had been waiting and for which the brigade had been prepared for many months. The brigade was led into the stockade by a young man on horseback, James McGill, aged 21. Like all his men he was armed with a revolver and knife and was resolute. An eyewitness, Rafaello Carboni, wrote of McGill 'You could read in the whites of his eyes, in the colouring of his cheeks, and in the paleness of his lips that his heart is for violence.' Carboni described McGill as being a small but alert man of good presence. He was short and not so much healthy looking as wide-awake. Carboni complained that McGill always seemed anxious to know what was happening but was not quick to volunteer help.

U.S. Consul Tarleton had been doing his utmost to persuade American citizens on the goldfields to stay clear of the stockade. He was anxious to prevent them from becoming involved in the bloodshed which would occur if events continued on their present course unchecked. The Consul's agent at Ballarat was believed to be a Doctor Kenworthy who did his best to pass on the message by circulating among the American miners. When the Independent Californian Rangers began entering the stockade Doctor Kenworthy was there to intercede with them. Other miners who were watching from a distance saw Kenworthy take James McGill aside for a long and serious conversation. They guessed sourly that Kenworthy was trying to persuade McGill to withdraw his men. However, the Rangers went into the stockade.

It was Saturday night, 2 December. The weather for that time of year in Australia was unusually cold. Many of the miners left the stockade to obtain better shelter back at their camps. Other men noted the scarcity of food and water in the stockade and the shortage of arms and ammunition and intelligently decided not to take part in the coming battle. James McGill placed about one third of his Rangers around the stockade on guard duty.

The miners' commander in chief, Peter Lalor, should not have gone to bed that night. As soon as he had disappeared into his tent in the middle of the stockade more of his army quietly dispersed. McGill also left the stockade with a large number of the Californians. Some said that he had gone to intercept the British army reinforcements known to be on their way to Ballarat from Melbourne. Another story was that he had gone to a nearby farming property to bring back a field gun owned by the landholder. However, Rafaello Carboni was to claim later that McGill deserted the stockade under orders from the U.S. Consul as relayed through Doctor Kenworthy.

Commissioner Rede and the local military commander, Captain Wise, decided not to wait for General Nickle to arrive with his reinforcements from Melbourne. They knew that they could take the stockade without a preliminary bombardment from the guns that Nickle was bringing with him. And in making that decision they were undoubtedly being humane. There was to be slaughter enough.

Just before dawn on Sunday, 3 December the assault on the Eureka Stockade began. The attacking force consisted of 152 infantry and 30 cavalry, reinforced by 74 mounted police and 24 foot police. Through the chill morning air came the ominous sounds of their approach – the snorting of their horses as they came through the white ground mist, and the steely scraping of sabres being drawn from their scabbards. Moments later sentry Californians crouching nervously behind the stockade saw the naked bayonets of British infantrymen glinting in the pale light and the dark skulking figures of the police bully boys sneaking up. The miners opened fire.

The first warning shots brought Lalor running half-dressed from his tent. From other tents inside and around the stockade came rushing other men only partly awake and shouting alarmed questions. The troops and police had begun shooting into the stockade and the cavalrymen were advancing at the gallop. To Lalor's horror he saw that of the 1,500 men who had manned the stockade when first it was built only about 120 defenders now remained.

The miners should have been in three groups. There were the Irish pikemen, supported by about thirty of the Californian Rangers, with another lot of men led by Nelson, the American carpenter; but within minutes there was complete confusion.

Surrender or retreat does not seem to have occurred to the miners in the stockade, possibly because they were not given time to think. Had they gazed around they would have seen the impossibility of defending such a large stockade with so few men. As it happened they were too busy fighting.

The Irishmen met the charging troops at the stockade, and the iron heads of their pikes clashed against the tempered steel of sabres and bayonets. The Irish fought with desperate valour and at first their pikes were surprisingly effective. But their manufacturer the German blacksmith, John Hafele, was one of the first to die. A cavalryman galloped over to where he was fighting, swung downwards with his sabre and clove off the top of his skull.

As their pikes were smashed some of the Irish grappled with their attackers. One of the Irishmen, Thomas O'Neil, was left sitting on the ground swinging his pike around his head. Both of his legs had been broken and he had received a critical body wound, but he continued smiting at all who approached him until troops finished him off. It was explained later at an inquiry that they had killed O'Neil because he would have died from his wounds anyway.

Nelson was shot in the thigh but crawled across on one leg to give assistance to his friend, Ross the Canadian, who lay dying, shot in the groin. Other miners were dragging Lalor away to conceal him from the police who were running whooping and howling through the stockade intent on massacre. Lalor had taken three bullets in his left arm, and his arm had been shattered.

The police bayonetted wounded and retreating miners, set fire to the tents within the stockade, and shot and killed some of the onlookers outside the stockade who had been non-combatants. They tore down the Southern Cross flag and ripped it into rags. A Roman Catholic priest, Father Smyth, kneeling in the bloodsoaked dust of the stockade beside the dying was dragged away by the soldiers. More than 100 prisoners were taken in and around the stockade, including men who had come running up from outlying parts of the goldfields too late to take part in the battle.

About thirty men had been killed, although it is probable that some of the wounded miners died later in hiding.

The American, Sam Irwin, who was watching, later described the scene after the carts had collected the corpses. 'They all lay in a small space with their faces upward, looking like lead. Several of them were still breathing and at every rise of their breasts the blood spouted out of their wounds, or just bubbled out and trickled away.'

Four of the soldiers had been killed, including Captain Wise, and another twelve had been wounded.

Ironically, the American-hating Rafaello Carboni, was arrested while attending to one of the wounded Californians. Carboni had been struck with the deepest of admiration for the man and the way he had fought. The Californian had six wounds in his body and all of them in front. Another of the Americans singled out for praise was a Negro from New York named John Joseph. Lynch, another of the miners' leaders later wrote of Joseph as 'a coloured gentleman who was arrested in the thick of the fight and who bore himself throughout the ordeal with a great deal of dignity.'

One who had lost his dignity was James McGill, now

a fugitive and with his Californian Revolver Brigade dead, wounded, captured, or scattered. McGill, dressed as a woman, passed General Nickle's troops on the road to Melbourne and made his escape in ignominy.

The rebel, Peter Lalor was still at large, and like McGill he had a price on his head. Lalor had been hidden by Father Smyth and was recovering slowly from the amputation of his left arm. Rafaello Carboni was in a prison cell, shackled to the Negro, John Joseph, and together with eleven other prisoners was on trial for his life on a charge of treason.

While the Crown had been preparing for the trials of the prisoners, the American Consul, Mr Tarleton, had been working with considerable diplomatic skill to obtain the release of all the Americans who had been captured at the battle of the Eureka stockade. Eventually he felt safe enough to send a despatch to the United States Secretary of State in Washington in which he blandly denied that any Americans had been involved in the uprising. His was a calculated diplomatic lie. This was borne out by a petition carrying 4,500 names which was presented to Governor Hotham in January 1855, and containing this interesting complaint: 'If His Excellency had found sufficient extenuation in the conduct of American citizens we thought that there were equally good grounds for extending similar clemency to all, irrespective of nationality; and that it was unbecoming the dignity of any Government to make such exceptions. ... We wish it to be distinctly understood by our American friends that we do not for a moment find fault with His Excellency for allowing their countrymen to go free, but we do claim, in sorrow, that he does not display the same liberality to others, that he does not wisely and magnanimously comply with the prayers of our petition for granting a general amnesty.'

Governor Hotham enquired: 'Were there any Americans at Eureka? I have not heard of it.'

A diplomatic row of the first magnitude would have followed had the story of James McGill and his Californian Rangers got back to Washington and London. Hotham had quite enough to explain to his superiors in the Colonial Office in London without making it worse. On the other side of the fence Mr Tarleton and his American merchant friends did not wish to endanger their business interests in Melbourne. Tarleton, and his successor at the Consulate Mr J. F. Maguire, were both active members of the Melbourne Chamber of Commerce, and could not afford trouble with the British Government. They conspired with Hotham to play down the American involvement at Eureka as much as possible, although earlier Hotham had been alleging that 'designing foreigners' had started the rebellion.

The blindness of Governor Hotham's official eye was demonstrated by the fact that the first of the thirteen prisoners from Eureka to be tried for high treason was the Negro, John Joseph.

Joseph was not an articulate person, but neither was he as simple-minded as he made himself appear. From the outset of his trial he maintained a disarming air of childish bewilderment and innocence as his best defence. With the hangman's noose in mind he played his part brilliantly, grinning foolishly and sometimes whistling before answering questions. Spectators in the public galleries convulsed with laughter. His trial became so ridiculous that it was useless to continue it, and the artful Negro was acquitted. His sympathizers cheered so loudly and long that the Chief Judge, Sir William A'Beckett obtained the arrest of two of them and sent them to jail for one week for contempt of court.

The second of the thirteen prisoners was acquitted without being required to offer evidence in defence, and it was recognized by the court that the jury intended to acquit all the other defendants too. The Attorney General secured an adjournment of the other cases, but one month later when the remaining eleven men were before the court each was in turn freed.

One day James McGill dropped in to visit George Train at his Melbourne warehouse. According to Train's later account of their meeting, McGill asked him to supply Colt revolvers to arm miners who were planning to continue the rebellion. Train wanted nothing to do with this and pointed out to McGill that he had become an outlaw with a reward of £1,000 sterling being offered for his capture. McGill said impressively, 'Mr Train, the miners have elected you President of the Australian Republic.'

Train told his friends afterwards that he was aghast when he saw that McGill was not joking about it. He knew that if word of this got out he would be in danger of arrest. His business would be ruined, and at the best he would be deported in disgrace. His sympathies had become too well known due to his past outspoken comments about republicanism.

The matter was hushed up and McGill dropped out of sight. Train declared long afterwards that he helped McGill to escape from the colony in a ship bound for England, but it seems more likely that the prestige of the American business community in Melbourne backed an approach to Governor Hotham on McGill's behalf. The Italian miner and writer, Carboni, said that he met McGill again in Australia about one year after the battle at Eureka, and reached a reconciliation with him. Carboni had been most bitter about McGill's disappearance from the stockade on the eve of the fight, but in the end he seems to have made allowances for his youth.

Mark Twain wrote that the people of Australia would keep green the memory of those who fell at the Eureka Stockade, but later Australians have much preferred to romanticize the criminal exploits of Ned Kelly and his gang of bushrangers. In fact many modern Australians are vague about the Eureka Stockade and are not too sure what it concerned. This could be a result of the British bias in the Australian system of education until fairly recently. Under this bias the history lessons given to Australian school children concentrated mainly upon the Empire-building exploits of Cecil Rhodes or Clive of India and of the European victories of the dukes of Marlborough or Wellington. Lessons in Australian history used to emphasize the intrepid journeys of early explorers and most of them British. Generations of Australians were led to believe that it was a calamity that the United States had broken free of the British Empire. Up to the Second World War the Australian school system was Empire-orientated and anything likely to tarnish the magnificence of the British Empire was not examined too closely. Australian schoolchildren waved Union Jacks on Empire Day and sang 'Rule Britannia' and celebrated at night with fireworks. Since then this British bias has diminished to the point of honesty – but even today few Australians have heard of the Independent Californian Rangers Revolver Brigade.

Karl Marx would have been disappointed in the Australian workers had he lived to follow their political evolution. The Eureka Stockade had laid the ground site for the construction afterwards of the Australian Labor Party and was partially successful in starting Australia along the road to self-rule, but progress towards political independence on a national scale soon turned into a long and sleepy country lane. Wise relaxation of controls by Britain proved too successful. British domineering mellowed into stiffly-maintained maternalism, a clever mixture of protection, direction, propoganda and assistance which lulled Australians into placid acceptance of the fact that many of their country's industries and much of the functions of political machinery which governed them still were controlled from London. The British monarchy was theirs, their highest judicial authority was the Privy Council in London, and all manufactured goods made in Britain and sold in Australia just had to be excellent and far superior to anything made locally.

The British had learned a lot from the American Revolution and did a brilliant job in emasculating nationalism in Australia. The fire of rebellion which had flared up too prematurely to lead to a republic was dampened down and subsided into ashes under which only a few embers remained glowing.

3

Americans and Canberra

When the Australian colonies formed their Commonwealth of States in 1901 their creation was an unsteady ramshackle of divided loyalties, rivalries and jealousies, instead of being an edifice of nationhood.

An American was one of the members of the first Australian Commonwealth Parliament. He was King O'Malley, the most flamboyant and picturesque figure ever to hog the stage of Australian politics – a poor man's Teddy Roosevelt who clawed his way to the top in almost everything he undertook, and who remained a spectacular extrovert throughout his career. He was to take a prominent role in the founding of the federal capital city of Canberra.

O'Malley had started his working life in his uncle's bank in the United States and later had become mildly successful in sawmilling and in real estate in Wichita, Kansas. In 1880, at the age of 30, O'Malley had migrated to Australia. He became interested in politics, and stood for the State House of Assembly for the seat of Encounter Bay in South Australia.

O'Malley had three manly promises to deliver to his gaping constituents during his election campaign. He undertook that if they sent him into Parliament he would legislate so that children born out of wedlock would become legitimate once their parents married. He also promised that barmaids would be banned from local pubs because they were a temptation to all decent family men. O'Malley further pledged that he would strive his utmost to have lavatories provided on passenger trains in South Australia. Subsequently, O'Malley received the whole-hearted support of illegitimates and their parents, and of wives with drunken and philandering husbands, and of everyone who ever had been taken short on trains in South Australia.

O'Malley had found the recipe for electoral success which many Australian politicians have followed since. Promises are effective when of a social or homespun nature and can be understood quickly and easily by the public without the use of much brainwork. They should also be delivered with some humour and a lot of rhetoric to make them sound both entertaining and professional. But O'Malley did not fail the people of Encounter Bay. Through his efforts all three of his promised reforms eventually became law in South Australia.

In 1911 when King O'Malley was Minister for Home Affairs his earlier dream for the building of a federal capital city for Australia similar to Washington was resurrected. The government selected for the site an attractive plain midway between Sydney and Melbourne, inhabited only by a few herds of sheep and cattle. It was on the fringe of the Australian Alps with an altitude of 2,000 feet. More importantly it had the strategic advantage of being more than 100 miles inland, and therefore being out of range of the guns of foreign warships. This had strong appeal to the politicians and public servants who would have to live there. Australia was still a devil of a long way from 'home' – which was Britain.

The Australian government planning Canberra had received good advice from architects in the district of Columbia in the United States, based upon experience gained from the failure of the original scheme for the construction of the city of Washington. A French engineer, Major Pierre Charles L'Enfant, who had designed the American capital, had worked under the close supervision of George Washington and Thomas Jefferson, but his ideas had been rejected or over-ruled too often. As a result, modern Washington was a travesty of what he had hoped it would be and bore little resemblance to L'Enfant's blueprints. It was an unlovely urban jungle which had overgrown the countryside far beyond the limits of the planning stage. In 1901, the United States Senate had appointed a committee to consider what steps could be taken to restore the city of Washington to its earlier concept, but after a full investigation the committee had found that it was too late and too costly to rescue Washington from indiscriminate development. However, it was not too late for Canberra and Australians could benefit from the Americans' mistakes.

Architects throughout the world were interested in the international competition launched by King O'Malley for a design for Canberra. Apart from having been a real estate salesman King O'Malley lacked any qualifications to be the adjudicator of the competition. When it was widely publicized that O'Malley intended to be the adjudicator the Royal Institute of British Architects, the Institute of Civil Engineers, and affiliated bodies within the British Empire nations boycotted the competition in protest. O'Malley and the Australian government refused to back down. O'Malley remained the adjudicator – although with the assistance of an expert committee of advisers.

A total of 137 designs was submitted – some terrible, some magnificent. By a majority decision the committee of advisers decided that Mr Walter Burley Griffin of Chicago, had provided the best design. The adjudicator, King O'Malley, then heartily endorsed this decision and declared Griffin the winner.

Griffin, who was only 34, already had some claim to being an international city planner. Earlier he had planned the reconstruction of Shanghai. He also had been a partner of the up-and-coming young genius, Frank Lloyd Wright, of Chicago. Most of his associates had been predicting that his future career would be more illustrious than that of Wright who had a more unstable character. They had good reason for this opinion. While Griffin had been industriously engaged on his winning design for Australia his former partner was somewhere in Europe, hiding from his creditors.

Walter Burley Griffin was a shy and artistic man but

his backbone was stiffened by his professional idealism and his vanity. The opportunity to design a federal capital city in the hinterland of Australia had for him great romantic appeal, and he also saw it as a chance to earn for himself a place in architectural history. Griffin was fortunate in having as his assistant a brilliant draftswoman, Marion Mahoney, who had been one of the first women to become an architect in the State of Illinois. She helped him with his design for Canberra and after it had won the competition they were married.

At the University of Illinois Griffin had learned of the mistakes that had been made in the planning of Washington. He had set out deliberately to avoid repeating them in the Canberra design. He had drawn up a city radiating outwards in a series of expanding circles from a central hill with a carefully planned road network becoming the skeleton of the future city. Griffin knew that this would ensure that Canberra kept its correct shape as it grew. In his plan he had provided for an adequate allocation of parklands and for a series of small shopping centres all within easy walking distance of each dormitory neighbourhood, as were also the schools.

Land and living space were cheap and plentiful in Australia and Griffin saw no reason why he should not concentrate upon providing a generous spaciousness which would make Canberra a city in which living would be as comfortable as possible with all community amenities within easy reach. The appalling ugliness and discomfort of Chicago, the cramped slums of New York and of other major American cities with their oriental overcrowding and lack of intelligent provisions for their citizens' happiness had been inexcusable for the New World. Griffin hoped that at least he could save the federal capital of Australia from such mistakes.

He foresaw Canberra as a city in which strict zoning would prevent factories and repair shops from intruding into residential areas, and which would also prevent overcrowding and overdevelopment in any one sector of the city. As the city grew the zoning plan could be repeated in other areas held in reserve by the Government. Thus the size of every self-contained district of the city would be kept in check, and the balance between residential, industrial and shopping and service amenities would be maintained.

But in the rustic Australia of that time not everyone had a high regard for the magnitude and splendour of Griffin's planning. Some believed that his winning design for Canberra was too elaborate. Others reached with a knife for the government's hamstring and alleged that it was extravagant.

Foundation stones for Canberra were laid by the Governor General, Lord Denman, the Prime Minister, Andrew Fisher, and by the Minister for Home Affairs, King O'Malley, and in that order of priority. Considering Australia's history, it was extraordinarily appropriate that an American joined the British Governor General and the Australian Prime Minister in that ceremony.

Holding a trowel made from Australian gold and with which he ceremoniously tapped the foundation stone, O'Malley engaged in oratory. He declared 'Our own evolutionary peaceable revolution that might have been productive of a thirty years war has been accomplished. Six independent States and territories are federated with one national government over all, so just and free that many wonder its achievement should have been so successful.'

O'Malley's speech impressed the colonials from Sydney, Melbourne and the bush who had assembled for this occasion. It made them feel that their country had come of age. At the same time the sight of Lord Denman standing there in his splendid British uniform reassured them that although they had become 'independent' in an isolated and God-forsaken continent on the edge of Asia, and 12,000 miles from the Mother Country, Britain had not forgotten them and would continue to protect them from all harm.

In August 1913, Walter Burley Griffin arrived in Australia eager to begin work. He had been appointed Federal Capital Director of Design and Construction in Canberra for a term of three years and with the right to have his own private practice in Australia. Griffin soon learned in bucolic Australia, however, that petty officials of all levels regarded him as being an outsider who had intruded into their domain of authority. History began to repeat itself. Griffin and Canberra began to undergo the same misfortunes that had befallen L'Enfant and the city of Washington. Griffin's Australian enemies set out to do everything within their powers to entangle him with red tape within their dusty little world, and to sabotage all his endeavours.

It would have been easier for Griffin to have abandoned Canberra and to have returned to Chicago to rejoin Frank Lloyd Wright in a more intellectually responsive, sophisticated and discerning society. He could have exposed the officialdom of Canberra to the rest of the world as backwoods yokels and smalltown hicks. But instead of surrendering and running back to his own kind as his wife urged him to do Griffin stayed in Australia to fight every move made against him.

The reluctance of the United States to enter the First World War aroused widespread anti-American feeling within the Australian nation. Griffin, an American in Australia, had to take some of the brunt of this. In Parliament one day a former Minister for Home Affairs, Mr Archibald, referred to Griffin as being 'a Yankee bounder' – an insulting British expression of that time with no reference to kangaroos. Archibald, a livid-faced Colonel Blimp, added for good measure that in his opinion the American system of doing business was to try to undermine others.

A Royal Commission was appointed to investigate allegations that there had been a conspiracy between Mr Archibald and senior Government officers to prevent Griffin from carrying out his duties in building Canberra. Witnesses established conclusively that buildings and municipal services had been constructed in Canberra without Griffin's approval and contrary to the city plan. Griffin's advice had been ignored and contour maps of the city's environs had been supplied to him by the Department of Home Affairs in the wrong scale. On one map supplied by the government to Griffin someone had wrongly marked a depression in the ground as a hill. The Royal Commissioner found that Griffin had been hampered wilfully and seriously in his duties, that necessary information and assistance had been withheld from him, and that his powers had been usurped by certain government officers. The Commissioner found that a hostile combination working against Griffin had included the former minister, Archibald.

A new Prime Minister, William Morris Hughes, ended the connection of both Griffin and O'Malley with Canberra. O'Malley fell out first with Hughes over the national dispute of whether or not Australian men should be conscripted to fight on the slaughter fields of France. Up to then all Australian soldiers in the war had been volunteers, but casualties had become so terrible that the Australian Army was in danger of being shot out of existence unless reinforced by conscripts. Prime Minister Hughes, a former Britisher, was in favour of conscription. O'Malley, a former American, opposed it. So too, did the Australian public. A referendum was held and Hughes' conscription proposal was defeated.

Hughes left the Labor Party to form a new political machine. He kept control of the Government, pushing O'Malley and others of his former colleagues into Opposition. O'Malley struggled on but was subsequently defeated in the general elections of 1917, and again in 1919. He was defeated mainly by the wider spread of anti-Americanism which had grown out of the war. Australians now were horrified by the calamitous losses that their army had taken in Europe. They claimed bitterly that had the United States come into the war earlier than 1917 their losses would not have been so great and the war would have ended sooner.

Walter Burley Griffin remained in Canberra after the removal of King O'Malley, but came into increasing conflict with Prime Minister Hughes. He consistently refused to obey instructions that he should accept compromises and change his city design. One day in 1920 the Prime Minister sent a brusquely worded note to him ending his contract after the expiry of the current term. Fortunately the further development of Canberra was retarded by diminished public funds during the two world wars and by the Great Depression in between. Meddling bureaucrats who would have ruined Griffin's design had they been given sufficient money to spend were kept in check. The reluctance of politicians and government officials to move to Canberra from their homes in Sydney or Melbourne also helped. Some temporary buildings and sheds were erected after Griffin's departure by people determined to turn Canberra into a typically dreadful Australian bush town, but luckily they were few. When the building boom began in Canberra after the Second World War more enlightened administrators recognized the true value of the American designer's work and staunchly defended his principles and plans for the city.

In time the city of Canberra became a remarkable success story. It grew as one of the few cities of the modern world to be rigorously planned from its earliest beginnings. Canberra has developed totally free of poor districts or slums. It has become a city of superb avenues, public parks and gardens – a city of man-made lakes and fountains, of comfort and convenience for the people who live there. It has become the city that Walter Burley Griffin of Chicago had dreamed of and had wanted to build.

After leaving politics O'Malley had formed a syndicate which had purchased one square mile of land on the north side of Sydney Harbour from Lord Carrington for £15,000 sterling. In later times the same area of real estate was to soar in value to somewhere around $A200,000,000. The Carrington family must still wince when they think of that sale in 1921. It does not fall far short of the sale of Manhattan Island by the Indians for a few beads.

O'Malley wanted to give Griffin an opportunity to show

what he could do with designs for suburban development. His syndicate formed the Greater Sydney Development Company with Griffin as managing director. The company developed the one square mile as a distinctive new suburb called Castlecrag.

Griffin offered five miles of waterfront of Sydney Harbour to the municipal authorities as a park, but incredibly his offer was declined. Local government was unimaginative and was incapable of visualizing the future. It was their fault that the five miles of waterfront offered to them as a gift to the public fell into the wrong hands and has since become crowded out by private buildings down to the waterline.

The homes which Griffin designed at Castlecrag and others in Melbourne were among the first built in Australia to satisfactorily cope with local conditions. They established a standard for modern domestic architecture in Australia. One of Griffin's inventions was the use of lightweight concrete building blocks which revolutionized the Australian building industry.

In 1928 Griffin told a meeting of the Theosophical Society in Sydney that the chief curse on the practice of architecture and engineering in Australia was that an over-balanced power of government had placed the shackles of mediocrity on individual freedom and scope of opportunity. He could have added that over-government and mediocrity was affecting all sectors of the Australian community. Progress had always walked with leaden boots in Australia. Mediocrity satisfied the easy-living and classless Australian people. Anything better than mediocrity was disturbing in their South Sea Island way of life. Those who displayed brilliance were a nuisance and were better off overseas.

In 1936 Griffin won a competition to design a new library for the University of Lucknow in India. His departure from Australia was unremarkable, except for the division of public opinion about him. He had made many friends and many enemies, and it seemed that for every person who wished that he would remain in Australia there was another rejoicing that he was leaving.

Griffin's arrival in India was hailed with excitement in that country. Within a short while he was building palaces for rajahs and had become a friend of Mahatma Ghandi. Twelve months later his life came to an end. He fell from a scaffolding on a building site, ruptured his gall bladder, and died from peritonitis.

King O'Malley survived to strut through the shining avenues of Canberra. In the Commonwealth Bank which he had helped to found were ample funds for his wants, and in his wallet was always a comfortable wad of the paper currency he had helped to introduce. At the age of 90, O'Malley gave his occupation in a census return as that of 'Bishop of the Water Lily Rock Bound Church; the Redskin Temple of the Chickasaw Nation'. He amused himself occasionally by exchanging insults in letters to the editors of newspapers with another ancient of Australian politics, William Morris Hughes, the Englishman. Sometimes, while making a radio broadcast as a guest speaker, O'Malley would recall some of his past exploits and from radios in widely separated parts of Australia would issue his cackling laughter. In December 1953 O'Malley died at the age of 95, leaving most of his fortune to charities. His indignant old widow went to court to claim an increase in the allowance that 'The King' had allotted to her. But O'Malley's judgement had been sound. His widow died soon afterwards with most of her inheritance still intact.

4
A land of mourning

Being a more mature nation, the United States had not
been as easily drawn into the First World War as had
Australia. American links with Great Britain were not
strong as were those between Australia and Britain;
American distrust of Europe was greater; American
knowledge of war, particularly derived from her own
terrible civil war, had made the United States cautious.
Initially, however, to many thousands of young Australians, the First World War had seemed to be a great
adventure, while to the high-minded it had been a crusade being led by Britain against evil. All the Australian
adventurers and crusaders who went to the war were
volunteers, the finest men of their generation. They de-
parted from Australia with exuberant enthusiasm, brim-
ming with cocky self-esteem – the native-born descendants
of Irish political rebels, American gold rush miners,
British free settlers, and the early convicts and soldier
guards. They were the A.I.F. setting out to conquer the
Huns. They would become the most aggressive assault
troops of the war. Every man loaded with initiative and
daring and high spirits. In 1914 these Australians could
not understand how the Americans could miss the opportunity to get into the war. It was going to be glorious.

Of course, the ever-present Australian desire to see
Europe was also behind that stampede to serve in the
wartime army. Every Australian of British descent wanted
to make the pilgrimage 'home' to the British Isles at
least once to reassure himself that he really belonged in
Australia and was not an exile as his forebears had been.
The war offered a free trip to find out. For a great many
of them it was their first and last pilgrimage. 325,000

volunteers went overseas to the war. Of these 213,000 became battle casualties. And at that time Australia had a total population of less than 4½ million. The flower of the generation was shattered. Australia had become a land of heroes, but too many of the heroes were dead. Australia had become a land of mourning.

The effect upon Australia was made more profound and lasting because the nation was too adolescent to endure such losses. Its history was too short, its traditions not sufficiently established to help its recovery. Australia was also too remote from the scenes of battle to permit its people to know if the carnage had been unavoidable. If they served no other purpose the awful losses gave Australians a sense of united nationhood which all the formal ceremonies and signing of documents only a few years earlier had not succeeded in doing. In addition a new attitude towards Europe, resembling that which had long existed in the United States, hardened in Australia. It was distrust. The Australian had been told that they had been needed to help save the world from the Huns and had believed it. Now they doubted that they should have been drawn into it. The war had been essentially a European quarrel. Some Australians declared now that their country had been used as a colonial recruitment ground for Europe, a fresh supplier of young men for cannon fodder. The shedding of their blood had not been of any visible benefit.

Disillusionment was most evident among returned soldiers who marched through the streets of Australian cities in the remnants of their legions on Anzac Day in the early years after the war. Anzac Day commemorated an allied landing at Gallipoli in the Mediterranean in 1915 – a military failure on a grand scale. The Russians had asked the British to open another front to take some of the Turkish forces off Russia's back. The scheme had attracted the First Sea Lord of the British Admiralty, Winston Churchill, who had recommended it to the British Government with all his eloquence and personality. Under the controversial leadership of a

British commander-in-chief tens of thousands of men made gallant but fruitless attacks against the Turks' defensive positions on clifftops which proved to be impregnable. The Australians had 27,000 casualties, including the death of their own commander, Major-General Bridges, before the allied army had to be evacuated by boat. But the Australian nation annually commemorated that defeat with the fervour of the ancient Greeks remembering their victory at Marathon. Gallipoli had become a symbol of bravery. This had been about all that the Australians had been able to salvage from the war.

On Anzac Day the returned soldiers who trudged through the streets of Australian towns and cities in bemedalled ranks were separated from the innocent clapping crowds and the weeping relatives of the dead by a chasm of awful experience they could never cross. Their eyes had been opened at Gallipoli and on the battlefields of France. They were pleased to meet old comrades again at their Anzac Day reunions, but their marches through the streets had a heavy-shouldered pretence of élan which was heart-wrenching to witness. They were but shadows of the high-spirited lads who had gone to the war believing themselves to be world-beaters. Always after the Anzac Day march a large number of the marchers went and got roaring drunk – many of them to forget the ghastly swindle which had been perpetrated upon a young colonial country of the southern hemisphere by an old and murderous Europe. Behind all the bugle-blowing, the massed church services of Anzac Day, the brightly polished silver and gold of the medals, the tramping of marching feet on bitumen roads and the cheering of the crowds, lurked something indefinable but sinister, something ugly. Afterwards, it was represented more genuinely by the drunkenness and flushed shouting faces, by the reckless gambling games in the parks and side streets, by boozy exhibitionism as the veterans took over the cities, by the solicitude of the wives who waited for their husbands to come reeling out of the pubs so that they could help them home, and by the later host of drunken veterans without wives to help them who sprawled helpless in the parks or were supported by comrades while they spewed into the gutters.

By that time Australians were admitting that the Americans had been smart to have stayed out of the war for as long as they had done. But they could not forgive them for it, and felt both superiority and contempt for all Americans because of this. In particular Australians found it hard to stomach the Americans' strutting and flag-waving, and their boasting that they had won the war. For Australians, whose own boasting had been knocked out of them, outrageous and offensive boasting became the trade mark of the United States.

5
The 1930s

Because of slack trading ties between the United States and Australia the crash on Wall Street in 1929 did not reverberate too noisily Down Under at first. The concussion came later when it rebounded from Britain. Australia's overseas borrowing almost ceased, partly because of the depression in Britain, and this severely cut the available spending power of the Australian community. Australia could not pay her debts in London – payments for imports and interest payments. With loans unobtainable and with export markets closing and catastrophic falls in prices Australia was soon in dire distress.

During the depression Australia made desperate attempts to get off the hook by increasing her wheat exports by eighty per cent in volume, by doubling her butter exports, increasing beef exports by a third, flour by a quarter and wool by almost ten per cent. She had great abundance of food and fibre when all over the world people were starving and were dressed in rags. But Australia had little money. Her greatly increased exports were down in value to only fifty-five per cent of the total sales of the same commodities in much lower volume before the depression.

For many years the nations of the British Empire had hoped to scratch each other's backs in trade. The British had believed that the Empire countries could provide British industries with a series of sheltered markets in much the same way that the consumer demand of the American States sustained U.S. manufacturers. In return the British sought to buy as much of the exports of Empire countries as possible. For example, she bought fifty per cent of Australia's exports in 1927, and these were mostly agricultural products. Under such Empire preferences Australia's primary industries were supposed to flourish while Britain's secondary industries would supply all the finished products that Australia required. (In more recent years, Japan with American co-operation has been trying to play the same game with Australia.) In 1938, Britain and Australia issued a memorandum admitting that imperial self sufficiency was a failure and that each country should develop home industries – which meant agriculture in Britain and manufactures in Australia. The trouble had been that British farmers had never lost priority of protection from the British Government while two of Australia's biggest rural industries, wheat and wool growing, had to have foreign markets outside the British Empire to keep them going.

Australia had never ceased to look wistfully at the U.S. market. For a long time the U.S. had been selling its products to Australia like a salesman dealing with members of his own lodge, but the U.S. had been reluctant to buy Australian products in return. During the slow emergence from the darkness of the Great Depression both countries set out to increase their overseas earnings, but the rapacity of the Americans angered the Australians. In 1934 the United States was buying from Australia only one-sixth as much as it sold to her. The Australian Government decided to get tough and introduced discriminatory duties, quotas, and import licences – directed against America. It took similar action against Japan who had been under-selling British manufacturers.

It was madness. The U.S. government decided that it could not permit a small country like Australia to kick it in the shins and get away with it. For two years, almost to the start of the Second World War, Australia was one of only two countries in the world not receiving 'most favoured nation' treatment in trade with the United States. The other country sharing this American displeasure was Nazi Germany.

Japan hit back too with disastrous results for Australia. She reduced her purchases of Australian wool by two-thirds and began to take a keener interest in synthetic fibres and other substitutes for wool. British manufacturers had thanked Australia for acting against Japan but could not make up Australia's resultant losses.

During the 1930s, however, an important thing happened to Australian industrialization. The U.S. motor vehicle manufacturers, General Motors, acquired the entire share capital of Holden's Motor Body Builders of Adelaide. In 1931 they formed a new company, General Motors-Holden's Pty Limited, which was to become famous in Australia and which pioneered the Australian automobile industry. General Motors-Holden's played a distinguished part in the production of an extraordinary range of products during the Second World War. It turned out engines, four different types of guns, air frame assemblies, and shell and bomb cases. It also made small marine vessels, tents, refrigerators and vehicle bodies. No plant in the country at that time could produce a finished motor transport vehicle.

An enormous American influence in Australia during the 1930s was the flood of Hollywood films which poured into the country. To Australians, Hollywood offered temporary relief from the worry of the Depression years – if they could afford the price of a cinema ticket. Moreover it introduced to receptive Australians an America they had not known. Australian audiences were gullible enough to believe the Hollywood portrayal of the U.S. and it made a heavy impact. Seeing was believing. George Raft, James Cagney, and Edward G. Robinson introduced Australians to American gangland, but most films of the era were wholesome comedies, musicals, romances or westerns to cheer up an impoverished world. The stars of Hollywood became as popular all over Australia as they were throughout the United States. Despite the current trade war Aussies got to thinking that any nation which could entertain them every Saturday night, and which could provide them with screen stars to love and admire and imitate, could not be all bad.

Words and phrases of American slang crept into Australian language and stayed there. Fashions in Australia followed those shown in the American films. Consumer demand was stimulated for material possessions displayed so matter-of-factly in the movies but often could not be satisfied because such goods were not available in Australia. For the first time, stay-at-home Australians were able to measure their own country against that of the Americans – and it fell short. This produced in many Australians a rueful admission of national inadequacy, superseding the aggressive rivalry which previously they had felt towards America.

Children crowded the front stalls at afternoon matinees, goggling up at the serials or shrieking over the clowning of Laurel and Hardy, or thrilling with the adventures of Tom Mix in the glorious freedom of the American wild west. And when they issued out of the movie houses, blinking, and saw the ordinary streets of the city suburbs in which they lived, Australia seemed by comparison horriby dull and flat. For them – as for many Sydney residents today – Australia started at Sydney Harbour and ended at the outer Sydney suburbs. They never really thought about the 2,000 miles of Australian wild west which extended right across the continent to the Indian Ocean.

The American films were so well produced, advertised, distributed and accepted that no other film-makers stood a chance. The few British films which got through to Australia at that time were apt to seem insipid and the acting in them pathetic. Australian film audiences had become conditioned so quickly to U.S. movies – to their stories and stars and acting styles – that they became impatient with any other. The amateurish Australian films, which local audiences had enjoyed, could no longer compete with U.S. films. And to drive home the last nail in the coffin rich American companies efficiently tied up cinema chains throughout the towns and cities of Australia.

Forty years later Australian film-makers were still battling to find any place where they could have public showings of their movies. By some obscure means legislation was passed by the New South Wales government in the 1930s which blatantly favoured the distributors of American films throughout New South Wales. This situation was brought into the open again in November 1971 when a new Australian movie, *Stockade*, could not be shown in movie houses or even in town halls anywhere in the State of New South Wales. It had to compete against U.S. films by being shown in Masonic halls or other private premises substituting for cinemas. The author of the screen play for *Stockade* was Ken Cook, a former journalist who knew how to raise a storm for the box office. Cook claimed that Australia had become a dumping ground for foreign film producers. He urged that some of the $17 million profit made in Australia by American film companies each year be siphoned off to help the Australian film industry. The wealthy and politically influential war veterans' organization, the Returned Soldiers League, took up the fight and announced a plan to show films in its national circuit of R.S.L. clubs. It promised that preference would be given to Australian films.

6
The Yanks saved Australia

In 1942 Australia became one of the first of a long series of countries to experience the turmoil, excitement and profit of having an American army in residence. Australian ports were crammed with U.S. shipping and the cities were packed with U.S. troops. A long period of isolation Down Under had ended.

The availability of Australia as an assembly and supply base was one of the significant factors in winning the war against Japan up to the dropping of the atom bomb on Hiroshima. A great American army trained and rested from battle in Australia during the Second World War, and from Australia, General MacArthur launched his successful offensive north through the islands to Japan. From his build-up of strength in Australia, MacArthur was able to employ the advantage of having much shorter supply lines to his forward troops than would otherwise have been possible. His short supply routes from Australia were also of crucial importance at a time in the war when the Japanese supply lines had become over-stretched.

Had the Japanese occupied Australia during their victorious onrush it is likely that the next area to experience the intensity of the Pacific war could have been the west coast of the United States. Sometimes people have short memories and forget their history and therefore there can be value in recalling what happened in the fairly recent past. Washington certainly should never forget the vital strategic importance of Australia in the Second World War or in any future major conflict embracing the Pacific and South East Asia.

The Japanese probably could have taken the whole of Australia within a few weeks early in the war of the

1940s had they known the full extent of their opportunity. So unprepared were the Australians to meet an attack against their own country in 1941-2 that they almost deserved to be conquered. In October 1941, when John Curtin became Prime Minister of Australia, he was shaken by the alarming situation which had arisen mainly out of the torpor and negligence of the Menzies Government which had been entrusted to run the country' during the preceding two years. Curtin made a survey and found that Australian industry was working at only fifty per cent of its capacity. Almost all of Australia's trained fighting men were with the British in the Middle East or in war zones elsewhere overseas in defence of the widely dispersed British Empire. Australia's Home Army was weak to the point of being non-operational. The few anti-tank guns available had only about fifteen rounds of ammunition per gun. The army had less than one week's supply of ammunition for its meagre field artillery. The army also had only six per cent of its total require-ment of rifles and only twenty per cent of the required number of sub-machine guns. New recruits had to drill with broom sticks, while on the beaches older men in the Volunteer Defence Corps went on patrol carrying cadet rifles for which there was no ammunition at all. Curtin also received a report that there was not one modern fighter plane in Australia. The Chiefs of the General Staff told the incoming Minister for the Army, Frank Forde, that if the Japanese brought one aircraft carrier to the coast of Australia and landed one infantry division they could capture the whole of the country. There were only a little over 5,000 men of the Permanent Military Forces left in Australia apart from the old soldiers in garrison battalions and in the Volunteer Defence Corps.

As early as 1937 the British had warned the Australian Government that Australia would have to rely upon its own armed forces and its own munitions if war came to Europe and the Pacific simultaneously. But Britain's warning had been as effective as a shout into the ear of the dead. At the end of 1941 the Japanese caught the

Americans by surprise at Pearl Harbour – but they did not need to use surprise tactics against the Australians. As a Christmas turkey waits for the axe so did the people of Australia wait for the advancing Japanese armies, unable to defend themselves.

On 27 December 1941, Prime Minister Curtin made it known that Australia looked to the United States as its only hope. In his appeal to America he said "The Australian Government regards the Pacific struggle as primarily one in which the United States and Australia must have the fullest say in the direction of the democracies' fighting plan. Without any inhibitions of any kind I make it quite clear that Australia looks to America free of any pangs as to our traditional links of kinship with the United Kingdom.'

By then American reinforcements, which had been intended for the Philippines, had already been diverted to Australia. Five days earlier, on 22 December, the first 4,500 U.S. troops and some artillery had arrived in four ships, including the heavy cruiser, *Pensacola*. Other American transfusions of strength soon followed. In northern Australia, airfields were built by Americans for U.S. fighter squadrons.

The first sight of an American soldier on Australian soil was hailed with tremendous relief by Australians as if everything now was going to be all right. A U.S. Marine band or the fluttering of an American flag in an Australian city was sufficient to convince the citizens that the mighty United States had taken over the protective role of Great Britain. There was a rising opinion that Britain had failed to live up to its obligations to look after Australia.

Australians were wrongly jumping to the conclusion that the Americans were coming to defend them because of feelings of warm kinship and a real interest in their welfare derived from past relationships and a common language. There was nothing altruistic about the Americans' new presence in Australia. The American nation had been following its policy of twenty-five years earlier by remaining neutral for as long as possible and had been making a hefty profit out of the war right up to the day that the Japanese had clobbered Pearl Harbour. The Americans were now in Australia because the U.S. army in the Philippines had been all but crushed by the enemy. The Americans were in Australia because they had no place else to go except home. It was much better for them to fight the Japanese in Australia than on the American mainland.

It was also ridiculous for Australians to think that the Americans felt for them in terms of kinship. Some of the Americans arriving in Australia in 1942 were the sons of migrants from Poland, Germany, Italy or Scandinavia, or were Negroes, and had no sentiment whatever towards former British colonies. Some of them were boys who had not even known where Australia was until it had been located for them on a map.

The war hit Australia before the cheers for the American arrivals had died away – and some of the Americans were among the first to be killed. Attacking Japanese planes got through to Darwin in northern Australia, destroying 24 U.S. and Australian aircraft in the air or on the ground within minutes, for the known loss of 5 of their own. Their bombers came over the coast and flattened the centre of Darwin and the waterfront area, killing 250 people and wounding 320 others, many of them civilians. They sank 8 ships, drove 3 others ashore and damaged another 10. One of the American ships sunk in Darwin Harbour was the destroyer *Peary* which went down with its guns still firing. As the sinking destroyer rolled over onto its side those of her crew still alive had to jump into the harbour which had become covered with blazing oil.

February 1942 was a month of unmitigated disaster for both the United States and Australia. The U.S. forces besieged in the Philippines were in the final throes of being battered into submission. The Australian Army which had been sent to Malaya as part of the Empire-defence concept had been captured almost to a man in the British base of Singapore where all the fortress guns were fixtures pointing out to sea – in the opposite direction to which the Japanese had come.

The Australian Government had been trying to tell Winston Churchill in London of the danger the country was in, but the response had been almost off-hand. In a letter which Curtin wrote to his wife on 5 January (quoted by Dr Lloyd Ross in his book, *The Curtin Papers*) the Australian Prime Minister bitterly stated 'The war goes very badly and I have a cable fight with Churchill almost daily. He has been in Africa and India and they count before Australia and New Zealand.'

Curtin had been demanding the recall of the Australian Army which had been fighting in North Africa and finally secured the release of two-thirds of it. Concentrating on global strategy Winston Churchill wanted to send some of the returning Australians to the defence of India, but was over-ruled by Prime Minister Curtin. Some units of the returning army, however, were sidetracked to garrison Ceylon. Others were put into Java where they fought against overwhelming numbers of Japanese invaders until forced to capitulate. The one consolation early in 1942 was that the U.S.A. was now on Australia's side.

One realist who had prepared for the worst was the military commander of the Australian Home Army, Major-General Sir Iven Mackay, who made ready to do his best with what little resources available to him. Being a skilful and veteran general who had lately returned from hard campaigning against the Germans in North Africa, Sir Iven Mackay had swiftly realized that he did not have the soldiers, arms, transport or even the ammunition to attempt to hold the whole of the continent of Australia. Therefore he made the cold-blooded but sound decision to concentrate his strength along the 1,000 miles of the east coast of Australia between Brisbane and Melbourne, this being Australia's main area of population and industry. General Mackay decided not to attempt to defend northern Queensland, nor Western Australia, nor the island State of Tasmania, with more troops than were already stationed there. As only a few battalions were in those parts of Australia they were as good as captured at any time the Japanese chose to land there. However, the Minister for the Army, Frank Forde, who had his electorate in north Queensland, rejected General Mackay's plan. He declared that the whole of the populated area of Australia be defended, but without explaining how this was to be done. Forde later denied right up to the age of 81 that the proposed 'Brisbane Line' was ever discussed by Federal Cabinet, but his denial seems to have been based only on a technicality. The author of a volume of the Official Australian War History, Dudley McCarthy, states on page 8 of the volume (South West Pacific Area – First Year) that General Mackay issued his memorandum recommending the concentration of defence forces upon Sydney with the outer flanks touching Brisbane and Melbourne. It was issued on 4 February 1942. McCarthy, who had full access to official documents further stated – 'Forde recommended that the Cabinet decide to defend the whole of the populated area of Australia.'

Whether or not Cabinet gave its agreement or discussed it was not really important at that time. Had the Japanese landed, Australia would have been placed under martial government and then General Mackay and not Frank Forde or Cabinet would have dictated the defence of Australia. Obviously, the sensible military plan – even though not desirable from a political point of view – was to hold open a beachhead on the east coast. ... And that was the situation when the Americans arrived.

On 18 March 1942, the American, General Douglas MacArthur was appointed Supreme Commander of Allied Forces in the Pacific. He was a fine military figure, tall and patrician and stern, impressive. The Australian public promptly adopted him as the standard bearer of offensive warfare and final victory in the Pacific. They rejoiced at the sight of him, cheered him and idolized him. He was, in fact, to be their saviour.

One of General MacArthur's own staff officers was to describe him afterwards as a brilliant, temperamental egoist – a handsome man who could be as charming as anyone who ever lived, or brutally indifferent to the needs and desires of those around him. The Australians, who did not get to know MacArthur well enough to dislike him for his faults, saw and admired only his obvious virtues. Foremost of these virtues was that he was one of America's most famous soldiers. He was a representative of the might of the United States, on their soil and preparing to defend them. In the war situation of early 1942 the Australians would have welcomed MacArthur had he been a man with a horned forehead and forked tail.

The first speech that General MacArthur made in Australia was a declaration of his war policy. It was nothing more than a brusque, austere recitation from a prepared script – but to the Australians it compared favourably with the oratory of Churchill and Roosevelt. It was part American corn, but also part deadly truth and all sincerity, however coldly stated. He said: 'My faith in our ultimate victory is invincible and I bring to you all the unbreakable spirit of the free man's military code in support of our just cause. There can be no compromise. We shall win or we shall die, and to this end I pledge you the full resources of all the military power of my country and all the blood of my countrymen.'

Australians carefully re-read his words in their newspapers, and thought over them. They were chilled by them, but at the same time comforted and heartened. Uncle Sam had answered Prime Minister Curtin's call for help.

The blind trust, however, that Australians so quickly developed for their new American leader was not at first well based. Like Winston Churchill the dictatorial General MacArthur had feet of clay. He was a wartime inspiration to the people he led but he was as warm as a block of marble. MacArthur was interested only in the final outcome of the war he was fighting. He did not have any lifesaving impulse to rescue the Australians from the depths of their own unpreparedness and stupidity beyond the requirements of duty and strategy. To General MacArthur, Australia was merely an ideal refuge from which he would begin a counter-attack northwards through the islands towards Japan. He was obsessed with honouring his personal pledge to return in triumph to the Phil'ppines. He yearned for revenge after his recent defeat there. He needed to erase the stain and humiliation of that defeat from his military reputation which was his whole life. Australia and its security were only incidental.

Australians tended to overlook that this impressive military figure stalking sternly around Melbourne was the general who had just lost his entire land forces in the Philippines to enemy action. He deserved dismissal, not admiration. MacArthur had been clearly out-generalled and out-fought by the Japanese. His timing in the Philippines had been bad. He had been caught off-balance by the Japanese. His handling of his air force in war had been so poor that a large part of it had been destroyed on the ground by the Japanese. During the onslaught between 6 January and 12 March, MacArthur had remained in his fortress of Corregidor most of the time and had failed to inspire the large part of his army fighting for its life on Bataan. He had visited Bataan only once. Furthermore, MacArthur had heaped abuse on the Philippines Air Force, and had accused the Commander of the U.S. Asiatic Fleet, Admiral Thomas C. Hart, of having run out on him.

MacArthur had left confusion behind him in the Philipines in his arrangements for the command of American forces after his departure. He had left Major-General Wainwright in command of only Bataan and of small pockets of troops holding out in the mountains. He had divided up the rest of the Philippines into three other comands under American officers and had planned to try to direct the operations of all of them from Australia. But he had not informed Washington that he was attempting and hoping to conduct the dying stages of the

Philippines campaign virtually by proxy from Australia or that he was not relinquishing his Philippines command. President Roosevelt and General Marshall in Washington assumed that Wainwright was in overall command in the Philippines and promoted him to the rank of Lieutenant-General on 21 March. On that same day MacArthur informed General Marshall of his own arrangements. Marshall and President Roosevelt both decided that these were unsatisfactory and confirmed that Wainwright was in command.

As a field marshal of the Philippines Army before the war MacArthur's preparations for the defence of the Philippines had been singularly unsatisfactory. As one of America's foremost military planners during the pre-war years MacArthur also had to accept part of the blame for not having prepared the United States adequately for its own defence. His lifelong preoccupation with the American Army from his childhood in an American fort through to his service in the First World War and later, should have made him fully aware that only the army which embraced new ideas and stayed modern remained on top. Somewhere in his middle years MacArthur's readiness to accept new ideas had slowed down. His receptiveness to change had set like concrete. He had become old-fashioned. His pre-war planning in the United States had shown that MacArthur had not fully appreciated the important role that aircraft and tanks would play in the wars of the future.

When MacArthur arrived in Australia he should have had trouble holding up his head. He had been smuggled out of the Philippines like a thief in the night, making the risky journey down to Darwin by fast boat and aircraft, leaving all his men behind, either dead or destined to become prisoners of the Japanese – which was probably worse than death for many of them. By comparison, General Gordon Bennett, the Commander of the Australian Army in Malaya, who had escaped from Singapore in a similar fashion, had returned to Australia to a court martial and was never forgiven. But when MacArthur reached Australia as a fugitive from defeat he was hailed as a hero.

General MacArthur's outward composure was an essential part of his public image. Upon him rested the responsibility of turning back the Japanese, and his behaviour was closely watched by the public and by his subordinates everywhere he travelled. To his credit he maintained an air of resolute calm and gave not the slightest hint of the sinking dismay that he must have been feeling. While the crowds of Melbourne were applauding MacArthur he knew that he had only 25,000 American troops under his command. Although he had ten times as many Australian men in uniform he tried to convey to Washington that he did not consider them to be reliable soldiers. He criticized the Australian militia as being an untried and only partly-trained fighting force. The militia made up two-thirds of the Australian Home Army. MacArthur stubbornly chose to ignore two pointed suggestions from General Marshall, his superior officer in Washington, that he should appoint senior Australian officers to higher posts in his command. On the second occasion he made the lame excuse that such officers were not available – which was simply not true.

The Australian militia were no worse than MacArthur's own green and inadequately trained units, but no doubt his criticism of the Australians was inspired by politics. He had to try everything to persuade Washingon to build up his American forces in Australia with all possible speed. He was a defeated general who had to be given another American army to try again. Also he had to compete for reinforcements and supplies against the requirements of the American generals in the European theatre of war.

In the early days of the Pacific War the battle-seasoned Australian troops from the Middle East just did not have a high opinion of the American soldiers, and this was noted by U.S. Lieutenant-General Robert L. Eichelberger who reported: 'Although Australian officers are too polite to say it to us they think that the U.S. soldiers are insufficiently trained and inexperienced theorists.'

It was not surprising that the American Army in Australia was insufficiently trained. In August 1940 the United States Army in America had totalled only eight infantry divisions, with one cavalry division and one armoured division. By December 1941 U.S. total forces had risen in number to 1,657,000 men. By April 1942 this number had risen again to 2,500,000 men. In the face of such rapid mobilization it was only to be expected that U.S. training of its army had lagged. The miracle was that the U.S. Army was able to go into battle so well equipped.

It was during that early period in 1942, when MacArthur was trying to strengthen his army in Australia, that President Franklin D. Roosevelt asserted that his preoccupation was with winning the war, and not with defending Australia or New Zealand. While the Australians had been lavishing hero-worship upon MacArthur the U.S. President had been worrying more about the progress of the war in Europe than in the Pacific. A biography of Roosevelt, written by James McGregor Burns, recounts that the President became so worried and so angry by the slow deliveries of vital supplies and other war materials to Russia that he told one of his advisers in a sudden outburst 'I would rather lose Australia and New Zealand than leave the Russians without American supplies.' It was another example of a hard fact which has continued to elude the political leadership of Australia – that America's global interests come first with the U.S. and that some of these American priorities are not always to Australia's advantage.

In August 1942, when an Australian army inflicted upon the Japanese at Milne Bay their first land defeat of the war, the Australian command displayed the coolness and professional skill of battle veterans while MacArthur and some of his staff in Melbourne behaved like nervous recruits. The Australian responsible for the defence of Milne Bay in New Guinea was Major-General Clowes who had fought in the First World War and more recently in the Middle East and in Greece. He had prepared his plans with speed and thoroughness and when the Japanese landed at Milne Bay he was ready for them. Clowes kept a large part of his force in reserve, slowed down and halted the Japanese onslaught with the remainder, and then threw in his fresh reserves for the counter-attack.

It was desperately close fighting with the Japanese infantry following their tanks through the Australian lines, sniping from the tops of palm trees and lying in ambush among their own dead. The Japanese rested by day and fought by night, attacking with great bravery and ingenuity. They tried to outflank the Australians at night by creeping along the beaches and wading out into the sea to by-pass defence positions. Amid pelting rain, mud and jungle both sides made savage bayonet charges culminating in hand-to-hand fighting. The Australian troops who took the initial brunt of the Japanese attack, and who held it down, were the much underrated militiamen. Middle East veterans then counterattacked, gradually overcoming stubborn Japanese resistance and driving the enemy back along the coast.

While the Australians were winning the battle MacArthur was seething in his Melbourne headquarters because he was not getting a ball-to-ball description of what was happening up there in New Guinea. Communications out of Milne Bay were poor, but MacArthur seemed prepared to accept second-hand reports. The Americans sent panicky messages based on inaccurate information to General Clowes, and made blustering declarations that he was not winning the battle quickly enough. They sent Clowes a foolish instruction to launch an all-out attack, although not having a clear idea of the current state of the battle. This so exasperated the Australian Deputy Chief of the General Staff in Melbourne, General Vassey, that he wrote in a letter 'We must know who commands the (Australian) army ... The sooner that is settled the better'.

The Americans at that time had little knowledge of the terribly slow and slogging nature of jungle warfare. Under such conditions prevailing at Milne Bay the battle was won by General Clowes' men in as short a time as was humanly possible. The Australian air force pounded the Japanese while they were trying to escape back to their ships, and the Australian infantry overcame the Japanese rearguard and hunted down the surviving stragglers who often fought fanatically to the last man.

In his despatches to Washington, General MacArthur was grudging and half-hearted in his acknowledgement of the Australians' victory – although it had been the first important Allied land victory of the Pacific war. Yet, when there was a move later in the war to depose General MacArthur from his post of Supreme Commander of Allied Forces in the Pacific, and to replace him with a British leader of the stature of Lord Mountbatten, the Australian Government stood by MacArthur and opposed it.

The Australian Government was as impressed by General MacArthur as was the Australian public. The members of the Australian War Cabinet particularly admired MacArthur's readiness to make rapid and momentous decisions and to stand by them. MacArthur attended most meetings of the War Cabinet and at their conclusion he liked to dictate in the presence of the Australian members his recommendations to be sent to Washington. Often these messages were couched in such imperious language that his Australian listeners wondered at his audacity. Frank Forde said later, 'No Australian general would have dared to talk to his Government like that.'

Forde felt such admiration for MacArthur that he sought the American's opinion on whether or not the Australian Commander in Chief, General Blamey, should continue to hold his command. Blamey was unpopular with his fellow Australian officers and Forde had been under sustained pressure from them to have him removed. One brigadier-general just back from the Middle East (later to become Lieutenant-General Sir Horace Robertson) was so confident that Blamey would get the sack that he walked into Army Minister Forde's office and coolly offered his services in any position 'up to and including that of Australian Commander in Chief'. When the worried Forde sought the advice of General MacArthur about Blamey the American gave it some thought before replying: 'Leave Blamey where he is. He's a good soldier.'

As the war progressed the grand strategy of the Japanese was revealed by captured enemy documents. They intended closing a net around Australia and New Zealand by occupying all the surrounding island nations. Already they had captured Indonesia and the Philippines. They were occupying New Guinea, and had invaded the Solomons. All that was required to complete the plan was the invasion and capture of Fiji, New Caledonia, and the New Hebrides. Australia was the prize within this island network.

During May 1942, the Japanese deviated from this plan by sending an invasion force by sea direct to Port Moresby and to northern Australia, their desire being to accelerate the pace of the advance. Their primary objective was the Australian port of Townsville where there was a large concentration of Allied shipping, newly arrived with American troops and war supplies.

Good Allied intelligence reports warned the Allied Navy Command in time. At top speed American and Australian warships got into a blocking position in the path of the oncoming Japanese invasion fleet. The battle that followed earned a place in history books as a new type of naval warfare. Not one shot was exchanged between the ships of the opposing fleets. The outcome was decided entirely by air power.

American and Australian aircraft operating from carriers and from the air base at Cloncurry in north Queensland compelled the Japanese to retreat – but not before Japanese planes had sunk the American carrier *Lexington* and the destroyer *Sims*. The Japanese lost an aircraft carrier.

That battle in the Coral Sea is recalled annually in Australia. It has become a symbol of alliance and friendship between the United States and Australia. Units of the American Pacific Fleet always visit Australian ports for the Coral Sea anniversary, and Australian officials receive the American visitors with all the honour they deserve.

The strange thing is that the Australian public has never put its heart into the commemoration. The anniversary of the Battle of the Coral Sea should be Australia's day of thanksgiving. It should be remembered as the day of deliverance from invasion. It was the narrowest escape that Australia has ever had.

Wartime censorship prevented the Australian public from receiving full information about the battle and the full fright and warning. The victory had been won out at sea beyond sight and sound of the Australian mainland, and therefore it became to Australians just another one of those battles fought in a faraway place. Few seemed to realize that it had been fought partly from Australian soil. It had been a last-ditch stand.

Anzac Day which commemorates a catastrophic defeat in a distant foreign land long ago continues to be observed annually in Australia. But the Battle of the Coral Sea commemorations are perfunctory and pass without much public attention.

As was to be expected, relations between American servicemen and the Australian population varied from good to bad under trying wartime conditions. At first the Australian public had seemed overawed by the glamour of the Americans. They had wondered at their fine uniforms which made private soldiers look like generals, and they had marvelled at the quantity and quality of American equipment. The Americans were like men from a superior planet. The poorly-uniformed and ill-equipped Australian soldiers often felt ridiculous in their presence.

All Australians had to admire the drive and bustle of American methods of getting things done. They were in a land where long official delays and red tape had been commonplace and where the pace of work usually had been slow – but the Americans would not tolerate delays or red tape.

Australian families invited the Americans into their homes. Others established canteen services for them in the cities, or arranged vacations for them in the countryside. The hospitality and friendliness reminded the U.S. troops of the small town areas of the midwest of the United States. The Americans discovered at once that few Australian women were used to flattery or to compliments and attentions which American women took for granted or demanded and received as their right. The Aussie women had been accustomed to living in a man's world, dominated by their men, and often neglected by their men. They glowed with happiness when they received small courtesies from the Americans – such as having car doors opened for them, or being presented with candy or flowers before a date. The Americans made the Australian women feel like princesses – and the Australian women avidly wanted to be taught more of the ways of a wider world than they had known previously.

Some of the repercussions were deplorable and sometimes tragic. The Americans found many Australian women who were lonely, their husbands or boy friends being overseas in the armies of the Middle East or in New Guinea or in Japanese prisoner of war camps, or killed. Sometimes an American visitor became the only man of the household. There was one reported case of an American sailor staying with a family in Perth who made three sisters pregnant and also their mother.

One of the Americans in Australia for a brief period was the trans-Atlantic flyer, Colonel Charles A. Lindbergh, who expressed his shock and disgust at the easy way in which American servicemen and Australian women got together. It became the impression of Lindbergh and of many other observers that the central city areas of Melbourne, Sydney and Brisbane had the world's biggest concentrations of whore houses. Lindbergh expressed the opinion that hordes of low-class Australian women were battening onto young American boys solely for their money — and of course he was partly right. Lindbergh wrote in his *Wartime Journals* 'We discuss the promiscuousness of Aussie women and compare conditions to those at home. Some officers are of the opinion that morals in Australia have always been relatively low. Others say that it is due to the war and that conditions are now just as bad — or good — at home. A major says that the American soldiers never meet the higher type of Australian girl because our men have carried on in such a manner that to be seen with an American uniform in Sydney practically identifies a girl as a whore'.

But the future was so unsafe at that time of war that youth felt justified in living only for the present. Many of the young Americans in Australia had just escaped death in the battle zones and would soon be returning there from Australia. They knew that next time in action they might not be as lucky. So they took every opportunity for a good time, knowing that it could be their last good time and that the women they were with could be the last they would ever know. The tension and impermanence of the Americans communicated itself to their Australian girl friends and was reflected in their social activities.

It was not until units of Australian fighting men returned home on leave and until the new Home Army had returned from training camps that there were sufficient concentrations of angry and jealous young Australian men in the cities to confront the Americans and to prove themselves.

Trouble between Australian and American troops on leave was played down by officials for obvious reasons, but it reached its peak in 1943. There were street battles in Brisbane which threatened to wreck the centre of the city before Australian and American military police got control of them. Fists, boots, belts and bottles were used in long and ructious mêlées while shopfront windows caved in and civilians ran for safety.

The people of Brisbane were almost as startled by the brutality of the American service police who went into the fray swinging their long batons at every head within reach and with an indiscriminate savagery that had not been employed in Australia in law enforcement since the convict era of the previous century. Their dazed and bleeding victims, Americans and Australians, were thrown into trucks for removal to hospital or lockup.

In north Queensland the soldiers in two troop trains – one full of Americans going south for leave and the other carrying Australian infantrymen back to the embarkation port of Townsville – stopped at signals and drew up alongside each other. The soldiers began exchanging friendly banter about women, and then insults, and then swarmed into each other's trains to fight it out.

These incidents were not reported in the censored newspapers but were spread through the camps by word of mouth, becoming more exaggerated with each retelling. They caused consternation among senior Australian and American officers who expected conflict between soldiers in full training for war, but who were concerned with maintaining efficient co-operation between the Allied armies. The Australian command closely investigated the causes of clashes between troops on leave and submitted a report which went to Prime Minister Curtin and also to General MacArthur. The report stated that causes of dissension included jealousy among Australians who resented the American's higher rates of pay and smarter uniforms (many of the uniforms issued to Australians had the style of clothing made from sugar bags sewn together by disinterested Afghan tribesmen). The report stated that preference given to Americans in the cities by taxi drivers because they had the most money angered Australian troops on leave. Drunkenness also had been playing a part in the brawling, but so too had the American habit of caressing girls in public, and their boasting and taunting to aggravate Australian soldiers.

On the night of 26 November 1943, the climax came outside the American Post Exchange in Brisbane, with an exchange of insults and threats between American military policemen and Australian soldiers. Like a Chicago gangster one of Americans opened fire with a carbine, at close range killing one Australian and wounding eight others.

The following night between 8 p.m. and midnight the city streets of Brisbane became the hunting ground for bands of Australian soldiers who attacked and beat up every American they could catch. Of those Americans injured eleven were taken to hospital, including four officers. Another ten were less seriously injured.

With such allies who needed enemies?

The Australian investigators deplored the American habit of drawing a knife or gun during a quarrel. Americans, when they became angry, had homicidal tendencies – like the Californian miners during the gold rush a century earlier. Australians, when angry, used fists or boots or occasionally a bottle, but in Australia only criminals used guns or knives.

The Australian Army carefully lectured Australian soldiers on leave about their nation's present and future relations with the United States, but General MacArthur rejected a suggestion that he should order similar lectures among his own troops. He said that Americans were too quick to detect propaganda and would not be persuaded by it. MacArthur also turned down an Australian suggestion that there should be some integration of Australian and American units for better understanding. The general's disinclination to co-operate was received by the Australian Army Command and by Prime Minister Curtin without official comment.

As a separate fighting force the Australians had been proving their value – even to General MacArthur. In addition to the Australian victory at Milne Bay another Australian army group had stopped the Japanese advance southwards through New Guinea on the precipitous jungle trails of the Owen Stanley Ranges only forty miles from Port Moresby. In Timor, Australian commandos had been fighting a tenacious and successful guerilla campaign against the Japanese army in occupation.

In the war zones relations between the Australians and

the Americans were cordial. Sometimes it was difficult to identify the troops of one nation from those of another. The Australians had gradually re-equipped themselves with a large amount of American clothing and battle gear which they had found to be superior to their own. They also had been going around salvaging damaged and abandoned U.S. heavy machinery and weapons, getting them back into service for their own use.

The prodigality of the U.S. Army both fascinated and repelled the Australians. There was the fairy godfather concern that its soldiers must have the best of everything, with the result that often, supplies classified by the Australians as luxuries were delivered to American front lines – and this, together with the abandonment of valuable machinery, weapons or vehicles with relatively minor defects, was the carelessness of the extremely rich. But sometimes there was also a terrible prodigality in men. American casualties sometimes seemed to be of no consideration in the winning of an objective. The U.S. was a big and heavily populated country and her generals occasionally gave the impression that they could well afford to lose good fighting men.

Most of the successful actions in which the Australians were engaged in the war gained their success because of close integration with the American machine support and with the back-up of American logistics and organization. Australian infantry guts and initiative and American air cover and organizational genius made a splendid combination in battle.

After the war 10,000 Australian brides went to the United States to join their American husbands. American boys who had been in Australia went home swearing that they would return one day to live there permanently. Most of them became caught up again in their home society and duties and could not return, but many Americans never got over their youthful love of the Australia they had known, and many years later were still yearning to return.

Typical of those U.S. veterans who could not get Australia out of their mind was William A. Kehoe. It took him twenty-one years to return. Kehoe had been a petty officer in P.T. Squadron 9, and had taken part in Allied landings from Guadalcanal to Okinawa. After the war he became a wealthy business executive in Oxnard, California, and put too much of his life into his work and home there to give it up. Eventually he solved his problem by establishing a second business and a second home in Brisbane. His Australian business, Forever Homes Pty Ltd, became as successful as was his business in the United States. In 1971 Kehoe's Australian business company gained a contract to build Ridgewood, a satellite town near Brisbane costing $A100 million. Kehoe had to divide his time between his home and business in California and his home and business in Brisbane, Australia. At last count he had made twenty-seven flights across the Pacific, commuting back and forth, but still undecided as to which side of the ocean he would finally settle for.

The Second World War proved that Australia's secondary industries could expand and diversify rapidly under the stimulus of a ready market for their output. All kinds of industries which were new to Australia were established and began making products from machine tools to locomotives, munitions and chemicals. Up to 1944 Australian plants produced more than 2,500 aircraft. Australians who had not previously believed their nation had many prospects of becoming an industrial country were agreeably surprised and pleased with themselves.

Just as impressive was the fact that Australia finished the war with a credit balance. She received assistance from the United States under Lend-Lease agreements to the value of more than £A300 million – a large sum at that time for so small a population to pay back – but in return Australia provided reciprocal supplies to the U.S. worth even more. Australia was the only Allied country to accept American Lend-Lease and come out of the deal with a credit balance.

7
Post-War: The lost opportunities

If the war in the South Pacific had been as static and had lasted as long as the Vietnam War the American occupation and the stimulation of danger could have transformed Australia into a great and dynamic country. But it happened that Australia received only a fleeting caress from the American god of prosperity and progress. Those who were to benefit from a fuller and more prolonged embrace were to be the enemy nations, Japan and West Germany. America's fighting ally, Australia, was left to fend for herself and lost her drive to succeed as danger receded.

America's fear of Russia and international communism was the motive behind the expenditure of billions of U.S. dollars to strengthen and stabilize the economies of numerous doubtful nations. Washington hoped that transfusions of money into sullen, wavering, backward, or defeated nations would transform them like magic into benign and trustworthy democracies. Everything in those countries would be all right once their peoples got a taste of *dolce vita* American-style and became consumers and customers patronizing a great world-wide supermarket. The Americans in occupation introduced foreigners to the excellence and profusion of American products, through generous gifts and loans, and through the payment of wages scaled to the higher American standard of living.

With American assistance Japan was lifted from the ashes of its burnt-out paper huts, and from its semi-mediaeval state, and was to become within twenty-five years more powerful and much richer than ever before. The same applied to all countries touched by the benevolence of American aid – but with one accord all detested their benefactor. Never before had a victor done so much to help the vanquished and the needy and been so reviled for it.

In those early post-war years the American Government and the American taxpayer were as gullible collectively as the young GI's who were fleeced by crooked taxi drivers and hotel doormen on their first trip away from home. Some of the foreign governments helped by Washington were no better than the Kings Cross whores who had flocked down to the Sydney docks to batten onto the wallets of American sailors every time a US ship came in. They exploited the American's paranoiac fear and hatred of communism for all that they could get out of it, and laughed up their sleeves. American aid often finished in the pockets of racketeers who frequently formed the governments of foreign countries. Frequently American aid resulted in the foreign rich becoming richer and the foreign poor becoming more pro-communist than they had been before.

During the decades before the war the American nation had kept to a policy of minding its own business internationally. After the war it was ill-prepared to take up the role of adviser and mentor to half the world's nations. The U.S. had little of the flair or the subtle skills in international administration which Great Britain had acquired during the last century and a half of her empire. The United States had to learn from the beginning and from its mistakes, but went at it with characteristic drive, playing God without human insight, without an exportable and acceptable philosophy, and with the objectionable assumption that loyalty could be purchased. The Americans began blundering with good intent along the road which led to Vietnam.

Australia was a 'safe' democracy, similar in many ways to the United States, and it was not surprising that the U.S. took her so much for granted. Yet, while Washington was so busy building free-world defences against communism, Australians had difficulty in understanding why the U.S. believed their country to be unimportant. After all, Australia was an entire continent, equal in size to the United States, all of it under one flag. Ethnically as well as politically Australia reinforced the United States. The two countries shared many common historic roots, spoke the same language, and had been regularly exchanging citizens and ideas for almost two centuries. After the Second World War Australia had remained one of the few nations deeply and genuinely grateful to the United States. Australians wanted to stay close to American power, too, and looked to the United States for leadership.

It was surely a crazy international policy which led America to help former enemies and neglect friends. Australia was a mighty producer of food and its large land mass had been only lightly settled. It was a country capable of enormous development but needed American aid to become organized and well-balanced. It was on the threshold of Asia and could have been made into a bulwark of the West. But the U.S. government looked elsewhere. Had the United States taken the Australian Government into partnership a small but strong 'America' could have been built in the southern hemisphere. The cost would have been only a small part of the treasure which the U.S. administration proceeded to pour so readily into more cynical parts of the world, and where much of it was wasted, or was likely to be used against Americans in the future.

The ease with which the United States could have transformed Australia is best illustrated by the fact that at the time of this book's publication a great surge of private American business investment in Australia had amounted to a total of about $US3.2 billion. Yet in the fiscal year 1969 the United States government handed out almost exactly the same amount of money – US3.2 billion in foreign aid, not including Australia. It had been handing out around that same amount every year for a considerable period, give or take a few tens of millions. And, although President Nixon later reduced foreign aid, the annual billion dollar handouts had not emptied American pockets all that much. $3.2 billion, even back in 1969, represented only 0.3 per cent of the U.S. Gross National Product.

Although without American assistance, the Australian Labor Party had rashly promised its country a Golden Age. It was a world in which all enemy nations had been disarmed and discouraged and in which Russia could not yet match America's military strength. It was an era in Australia in which the present was all-important and the future not worth a second thought. There would be floral leis and hulas all around for ever and ever and Australians would receive rewards without having to worry too much about earning them. In fact, Labor's promise of a Golden Age had been only stating an established condition. Already Australians had attained a way of life for which the peoples of other nations had been striving since the beginning of history and for which terrible wars and revolutions had been fought. Theirs had become a classless society governed by the common people. Theirs had become a society in which poverty was rare. Prime Minister Chifley should have been concerned with galvanizing his people into an awareness of their great and rare good fortune, and into determined endeavours which would ensure that their children and grandchildren also would enjoy it.

During those first post-war years of reconstruction, sunshine and fun, no further attention was paid to national defence. The air force which had been equipped with the world's most modern aircraft dwindled to a few squadrons of obsolete planes. The Australian aircraft industry which had produced war planes was shut down so that the country henceforth had to purchase all its aircraft overseas, much to the gratification of U.S. and British aircraft manufacturers. The Australian Navy, which had fought so magnificently during the war, was reduced to a few aged warships of small value. The shipyards which had been building navy vessels contracted in their activities and were not turned over to the construction of a much needed merchant fleet. Australia's trade remained at the mercy of foreign shipping combines which charged high freight rates. Two years after the war the northern and western areas of Australia – which a Labor war minister had been prepared to defend to the last ballot box – had become defenceless again.

The United States had offered an excellent opportunity to build up a permanent defence base at Manus Island north of Australia, but the Labor Government passed it up. Manus Island had been a main base for the American advance to the Philippines. Its lagoon had provided safe deep-water anchorages for up to 2,000 invasion ships at once during preparations for the offensive. Extensive shore installations had been constructed. The U.S. government had suggested that Manus should become a permanent base for the United States Pacific Fleet and for the miniature Australian Navy. The Australian Government, however, turned down the offer, principally due to the opposition of Dr Evatt, who was then a senior minister in the Government. An American base at Manus Island would have given Australia the northern protection it later sought. It also would have made it easier for the American Navy to have operated 'around the corner' in the eastern Indian Ocean and close to Indonesia. But the Australian Labor Government was too full of nationalism to see the advantages of the proposal or to admit to the realities of the situation even to themselves. The Labor leaders wanted Australia to be defended by its powerful friends and allies, but like other former British colonials they did not wish to see their country freed from the British harness only to have an American yoke replace it.

A smart U.S. administration could have found a way to use this nationalism without offending it. Joint ventures with the Australian Government in planning further development within Australia with the assistance of U.S. technology, loans and trade preferences could have increased Australia's industrial and economic strength further. It would have made the country more self-sufficient and self-generating, and again able to repay its debts once growth had been achieved. It would have been good business. Instead, the U.S. government took rebuffs like the Manus Island refusal as an indication that the Australian Government did not want help, and backed off. The Australian nation was left to go it alone like an orphan turned out into the street. The British were no longer of any assistance to Australia. The British were so broke that Australians were sending them food and comfort parcels. Australia had become a refuge for the British.

One of the first big American companies to see the new opportunities in Australia – even if the U.S. Government could not – was General Motors-Holden's. At the invitation of the Australian Government it became the first company to manufacture motor vehicles in Australia. By 1970 U.S. shareholders were getting up to $A27 million annually on that deal – and for Australia one of the most serious deficiencies of Australian industrial production, as had been highlighted by the recent war years, had been overcome. U.S. private enterprise was ready at a price to help anyone.

In 1949, a Liberal-Country Party coalition government took over Australia from Labor. It was led by the lucky Robert Menzies – lucky in that his countrymen were of short memory and were disinterested in politics or national problems that did not immediately affect their happiness. Changed circumstances, the lapse of seven or eight years, and his own political shrewdness had permitted Menzies to get up off the floor and to clamber back onto the top perch again. Menzies was such a quick-witted fellow and such an amusing public speaker that he won many new admirers, both in Australia and in the United States. Throughout this second long term in office he covered over his many mistakes and omissions with his urbanity and his ability to mock and ridicule his critics. Because of this he received much more public tolerance and admiration than he deserved. He was without the genuine qualities of statesmanship. His vision of the future seldom seemed to extend further than the next elections and usually he gave top priority to the requirements of the Liberal Party and to the constant need to placate its partner, the Country Party, to hold the coalition together. His harshest critics saw Menzies as a drum-thumping brass band leader, heading out across a strange city on a random route and without a street directory in his pocket – which did not really matter because he had no particular destination in mind.

In the 1960s and the 1970s American companies working in the remote and empty north and west of Australia often wondered what sort of fools had been running the country in which they were operating. Development of quite rich and fertile areas of the nation had been left entirely to fate and foreign investors. There was an American word called decentralization which was often used in the Australian Parliament but its use had been meaningless. It was an emotive word which Australian State governments used to squeeze more money from the Federal government when it had become necessary to win over voters in this rural electorate or that. It had no true relationship to national planning. The Federal dispensers of 'decentralization' money scattered a little this way or that like farmers feeding wheat to chickens. Decentralization had no true relationship to national planning.

Almost invariably coalition governments are inept, unsatisfactory and makeshift administrations in which politics have to take precedence over government. Prime Minister Menzies was virtually the prisoner of his coalition which lasted until his retirement seventeen years later and then longer. A post-war boom strained the Australian economy while the people were being given what they had been denied during the war years, and there had been a great release of national and public spending. But expediency and party politics ruled in Australia, and even after postwar reconstruction had been completed by 1955 the Government seemed to be without any real sense of purpose.

Australia was not an easy, fertile country to settle from coast to coast as the United States had been, and it had less time before foreign controllers stepped in. Responsible government in a vast and under-developed country such as Australia demanded the fixing of national targets for the people to achieve and the planning of a rational development timetable. No Australian government could order people in peace-time into parts of the country where they did not wish to reside, or into jobs which they did not like, but the Federal government of Australia held central control of the country's revenue. It had the financial power to make it attractive for young people and migrants and industries to transfer to the north of Australia or to any other habitable part of the nation, and to sustain them there until they had become established. By the same means it could have made the unhappy over-development of Australia's southern and eastern capital cities more difficult. Such direction was of particular importance at a time when Australia's immigration scheme was bringing great numbers of new settlers into the country every year, and when an inordinate share of the national wealth was being poured into the capital cities.

After 1950 about 25 per cent of Australia's Gross National Product was saved and invested in factories and public works intended to help develop Australia. This was about the same proportion as in the United States. However, as Professor Shaw of Monash University pointed out in his survey, *The Economic Development of Australia*, the true test lay in whether or not the money had been wisely spent. He found that not nearly enough of Australia's money had been spent in vital sectors. Transport facilities remained inadequate and money spent on education in Australia remained low by international-advanced nation standards. In 1958 Australia was spending only 3 per cent of her Gross National Product on education. Only 28 per cent of young people aged between 15 and 19 in Australia were being educated full-time compared with 66 per cent in the United States. In

Australia only 1.9 per cent of the population received a tertiary education, compared with 12 per cent in the United States.

In 1956-7 road transport in Australia was responsible for more than 25 per cent of the total passenger miles performed, and for more than 25 per cent of the total ton-miles of goods carried. Yet in the following seven years less than 3 per cent of the national income was spent on roads and bridges – nor was this increased much later. The coalition government could argue that it could not be expected to do everything for Australia all at once, but in some vital sectors it did not seek to do much at all. It seemed content to permit the people of Australia to make their own way as best they could and with an occasional pat on the head to reassure them that Canberra was still there. In the United States internal conflicts and competition had spurned on private enterprise to settle and develop the country. In Australia there was a marriage of aimless drifting and monopolies. Prime Minister Menzies solidified into a national figurehead of inactivity like a smiling bronze Buddha.

In international affairs Menzies had quite the opposite outlook to that of the Australian Labor Party. He was not a nationalist of conviction. He had been so Empire-indoctrinated in his early youth that he always stayed a colonial in essence. He was one of the last people to accept that the sun had finally set upon the British Empire. Only when the British delivered a rude shock to him by announcing that they were going to withdraw their armed forces from Asia did Menzies awaken with a jolt and begin thinking about obtaining protection from the United States. Not technology nor aid for industries from the United States. Not help in building new ports and towns in remote areas for better population growth and distribution and ultimately defence development – he just wanted protection. As John Curtin had done, Prime Minister Menzies, with less justification, turned to persuade the United States to take up the shield which

Britain had dropped and behind which Australians had become over-fed and vulnerable city-dwellers.

It became part of the misfortunes of President Lyndon Baines Johnson that the Menzies coalition government was still in power in Australia during the 1960s. It was then that President Johnson began looking around for allies to make the U.S. incursion into Vietnam more presentable to the rest of the world. Had a Labor government been in control of Australia at that time President Johnson would not have received any encouragement from Australia to enlarge the existing war in Asia. It is just possible that a better Australian government could have helped the United States out of Vietnam a lot earlier.

8

The Vietnam confidence trick

The word 'communism' still produced in America the dumb panic which the late Senator Joe McCarthy had been able to exploit and which Castro had renewed. Emotional abstractions such as 'the domino theory', 'militant communism' and 'international revolution' were in popular use without everyone being sure of their meanings. They were part of modern democratic jargon. Such abstractions in mass communications were as confusing and unreliable as was the communist countries' claptrap about 'revisionistic bourgeois ruling circles' and 'imperialist running dogs'.

According to the domino theory every Asian country which caught a dose of militant communism was likely to infect the next one across the border and bring on an epidemic of international revolution. Russia and China were forcing the virus down the throats of the peasants of South East Asia and, unless something were done to isolate it, the infection would travel south to Australia like Asian flu.

In 1965 few Western leaders had tried to review the political realities in China and South East Asia from the viewpoint of the peoples of those countries. These Asians had been lagging in their social and economic development 1,000 years behind the progress of the West. The illiterate peasant masses of Asia were barely aware of the names of the countries in which they lived, so fully occupied were they in staying alive. Every year famine and disease killed off millions of them before they had reached middle age. The introduction of Western medicines stopped some of the diseases, but helped to produce even more calamitous increases in population and food shortages. In 1965 many Asian peasants had even less to lose than had the Russian peasants of 1917.

Usually, Asia's revolutionary leaders were nationalists who were trying to drag their peasant countries by the scruff of the neck into the 20th century. They were not interested in joining either Russia or China in any grandiose scheme for an international communistic revolution to save the world, but were willing to accept instruction and assistance from them to awaken Asia from its centuries-long slumber. The revolutionaries were opposed by despots supported by a rich and well educated élite who had been enjoying their lives while millions of their countrymen suffered and starved. A fortunate few had been in control of Asia every generation throughout the centuries. They had permitted abysmal poverty and ignorance to continue with studied indifference and for self-preservation – as had the European lords of the Middle Ages. Now time was running out for them, just as it had run out for the noble families and rulers of pre-revolutionary Russia and France and China. They would be the first to have their throats cut if a peasant revolution succeeded. They knew it, and most of them were prepared to fight to the last American to keep the revolutionary peasants down and to save their own lives and property and power.

The experienced British had realized that the awakening of Asia was an irresistible current of history. It could not be prevented by fighting ruinous and futile wars against people who were becoming implacably determined to run their own affairs. But the equally experienced French and Dutch had not wished to believe that Asia would no longer tolerate foreign overlords. The French and Dutch remained in Asia to fight. The people defeated them and swept them out of Asia.

If the various peasant countries of Asia, being awakened one by the other, wished to use communism as a vehicle into the 20th century, two actions were certain to accelerate the process. One was to supply money and arms to the old ruling order which had nothing in common with the people, no matter which way the votes were stacked. The other and more certain method was for a capitalist Caucasian country to put its own troops into Asia to fight against revolutionary nationalists who were being supported morally and materially by communist countries.

Asians had seen too many foreign armies on their soil. They backed their own kind against Caucasians every time, and more particularly intense was their opposition if the round-eyed intruders aligned themselves with the old order.

In Vietnam and in other Asian countries the United States – and Australia – had an infallible instinct for taking the wrong side. Being rich and conservative nations they felt impelled to give their help and sympathies to the established despots who were doomed to be defeated sooner or later no matter who tried to prop them up. In taking the wrong side the Americans and Australians were opposing the people of Asia. The United States had become so emotionally misled by the label 'communism' that it had completely forgotten that America too had been a revolutionary nationalist country and had sought to sow the seeds of rebellion abroad for the benefit of oppressed peoples.

The classic example of the weakness of so-called international communism as a world force had been provided by the gulf of enmity which had opened between Russia and her protégé, China. Eventually nationalism would always prove stronger than the theories of communism, and what was suitable for one communist country was not often acceptable to another. The spectre of universal agreement between communist countries was not likely to rise. Communism, however, was a step up the ladder for a country escaping out of feudalism, and it was the easiest step for nationalists to take while rallying their peasants. Communism was harsh medicine to be forced into the guts of nations when they were prostrate and it frequently had a crude and simple appeal to a crude and simple people. It was also exportable to other countries with similar desperate problems of inequality, ignorance and poverty. It was a base political system.

The U.S. government feared communism in all its forms far too much. It never seemed to understand that compromises and concessions always have to be made to meet changed circumstances. Communism always had to change after revolution succeeded and as a nation became wealthier and its people better educated and better housed, better clothed and better fed. It followed that communism varied inevitably from one country's version of it to another's, according to development, enlightenment and temperament. Communism was an evolving political system like all others. It was no more likely to succeed as a unifying international brotherhood than any other Utopian pipedream. It carried within itself the nucleus of its own destruction, its tyranny.

The United States had been encouraged in Asia by the 'westernisation' of Japan, South Korea, and Taiwan, but the U.S. should have realized that it was too dangerous and too expensive for even the world's most powerful and richest nation to attempt to subdue and finance other Asian countries into a similar facsimile of American democracy – especially when nationalism would eventually prevail no matter what happened.

Most countries in Asia were not in fact ready for democracy in the American style. It was not an exportable product like Coca-Cola or popcorn. American democracy ran on the well-greased wheels of capitalism and private enterprise and on the general acceptance and enforcement of laws which had taken a long time to establish. It presumed, often wrongly, that most of the nation's people were capable of making the most of their opportunities and could look out for themselves in a fiercely competitive commercial world. But the more efficient and aggressive the employers in a democracy, the better educated the workers had to be to look out for themselves and to obtain for themselves a fair share of the national wealth. The mass of Asians were not prepared for the American system. For that matter, even the Australians were not sufficiently prepared for the American system.

The American conception of politics in a democracy

was also too rich a diet for the Asians. The more representative the political system the more politically sophisticated the people had to be to exercise their rights and to
understand their responsibilities and to protect their
power. The peoples of Asia were mostly too backward –
through no fault of their own – to cope with American-
style politics. It was like trying to graft the head of a
lion onto the underfed body of a goat.

Australia was a brash New World nation like the
United States with even less understanding and perception than the Americans in foreign affairs. But the Australians had been given expert advice by the British –
to whom they listened – that it was folly to become
embroiled in the war in Vietnam. That advice should have
been passed on by Australia to the United States. Australians had a moral obligation to repay the debt they
owed the United States for services rendered during the
Second World War. Unfortunately only petty politicians
and yes-men were available in Australia to counsel the
Americans at the time when crucial decisions were being
made over Vietnam.

After the Menzies Government had given the United
States its fullest verbal agreement and encouragement for
the escalation of the Vietnam War it should have given
America its fullest military support. Instead of doing that
the Menzies Government revealed the extent of its in-
sincerity by giving only one battalion of infantry to help
fight the war. At no stage had the Australian Government
any intention of making a truly strong effort. The Australian involvement in the war was only half-hearted and
an obvious sham to win favour with a great and powerful protector. The Australian people had not been con-
sulted in advance. The Menzies Government had sidled
them into the war by stealth and deceit. Its pretence that
the South Vietnamese government had appealed to
Australia for help did not fool anyone.

The Australian people had learned from the two world
wars and from other conflicts that military adventures
thousands of miles from home did not pay off for a small

country like theirs. Their place was at home. Politicians and generals could talk of the value of forward defence until they were black in the face but the Australian people had had enough. No more would they eagerly volunteer to campaign abroad and risk getting themselves killed in someone else's country. The expeditionary force glamour, the trumpeting crusade, the call to military adventures had been used on them too often over too short a period.

On 7 August 1964, a Senate resolution had given the United States President the authority to use armed force to assist any member country of the South East Asia Treaty Organization to defend its freedom. The wording of that resolution had in it something of the ringing grandeur of a speech by Abraham Lincoln. It had been the resolution of a fine nation still proud of its strength and good intentions. It had been a resolution not lightly made nor likely to be soon repeated. It had been a resolution which the Australian government, as a member of SEATO, should have wanted reserved for a future crisis more dangerous to Australia than the Vietnam struggle.

Non-combatant countries settled back to watch the world's most powerful nation, the United States, biting off more than it could chew in Vietnam. Former enemy nations which had been defeated and later restored by America secretly gloated over the spectacle of the Americans being defeated and humiliated in Vietnam. Former allies of the United States also stood by and watched with malice, not offering help. They were remembering the tardiness of the United States in entering the two world wars and the profiteering of the Americans during their wartime anguish. They saw retribution in the Americans being trapped at last and being forced to fight while others prospered.

Of all the nations Australia was in the least creditable position. The Australian government, with its warlike declarations of support for America, and its token assistance, tried to bluster through. A substantial protest movement built up among the Australian people and their own government tried to discredit it – but gradually lost credibility itself.

It had stuck in the craw of the Menzies Government that Britain had decided against sending even a token force to Vietnam. Menzies' successors grumbled that Australia had helped Britain fight her wars in Europe as well as in Asia. Paul Hasluck, a Menzies' man, put it this way: 'It is the Australian view that West European nations interested in a continuing part in world affairs must play a continuing role in Asian affairs.

'The phrase – "peace is indivisible" – is true when trouble is most likely to break out in Europe. It it no less true when the most immediate threat to world peace is in Asia.'

Hasluck had a great deal too much to say on behalf of his country which had put only 8,000 men into the war in Vietnam. His lecture to the British, who had been displaying a masterly understanding of the Asian situation, smacked of impertinence. Hasluck also revealed that he had little sensitivity for France which had lost so many of her best soldiers in fighting a similar war in Vietnam, although for different reasons. His words sounded reasonable enough to the Australian electorate which was their main target.

President Johnson's visit to Australia in the latter part of 1966 was partly designed to focus the attention of the American people on the alliance with Australia for his own political purposes. But it was also designed to help a sympathetic Australian government to remain in power. With this in mind he became the first American president to campaign in an Australian election. Possibly the Labor Party, which was being led by the unpopular Arthur Calwell, would not have won the election anyway, but President Johnson's personal call to visit Prime Minister Holt in Australia as a supposedly grateful war ally just before the election was so successful that it put the election result beyond doubt. The post-war prestige of the United States in Australia was at its peak and

President Johnson conveniently symbolized the United States. Australians felt flattered and honoured that an American president still in office should think their country important enough to visit, and they turned out in their hundreds of thousands to cheer Johnson through the streets in scenes of hero-worshipping enthusiasm never before seen in Australian cities.

It was Johnson who received the Australian bouquets which were not produced for the U.S. during the annual uninspiring commemorations of the Battle of the Coral Sea. The generation of Australians who felt themselves most in debt to the United States expressed their feelings in one outburst to the U.S. President when he went to see them in person. The younger demonstrators against the Vietnam War, who lay down in the streets and who threw red paint over the President's car, and who struggled against the police and the presidential bodyguard, were in the minority. They could not detract from Johnson's triumph.

Johnson's popularity in Australia generated a greater public warmth for Prime Minister Holt, his friend and close companion during the visit, and Holt's coalition government was later returned to office in a landslide electoral victory. The aged Labor leader, Arthur Calwell, who had promised to withdraw all Australian troops from Asia if he became prime minister, lost the leadership of his Party. Calwell, the gravel-voiced grandson of an American miner, resented the intrusion of the American President into Australian politics, but suggested another reason why Australians had returned a pro-war government. Calwell rasped: 'They were afraid.'

If Australians truly had feared that their country was in any danger they surely would have volunteered to form a large army to help the Americans fight in Vietnam. No such volunteer fighting force could be raised. The Holt Government had to resort to recruiting youths aged 20 by conscription ballot to keep the small Australian contingent in Vietnam up to full strength. The ballot was a lottery of birthdays strongly opposed by the antiwar factions and condemned as unfair by those whose numbers were drawn. Those caught in the lottery-draft had to risk their lives in a hot, dirty and miserable little country in South East Asia while other young Australian men of their age were able to continue enjoying themselves at home as if Vietnam did not exist. Some youths chose to be jailed rather than be drafted into the army. The warrior tradition of an earlier Australia had become hollow – and this was partly due to the over-emphasis by the Australian Government in recent times on the need for U.S. protection.

One bizarre episode arising out of the opposition of numerous Australians to the war involved Fred Moy – a man with a Chinese-sounding surname but whose ancestors had been Irish. Moy, who was a farmer in northern New South Wales, was a veteran of the Second World War and was blind in one eye. He was not a member of any political party but decided that not enough had been done to settle the Vietnam conflict by negotiation. Painstakingly he drew up a seven-point peace plan which he believed to be fair to both North and South Vietnam, and to the United States and also to Australia. Then he went to Hong Kong at his own expense and delivered his peace plan to Chinese government officials whom he contacted through the Bank of China.

Behind the scenes there must have been considerable ferment with the Chinese trying to discover if the presentable and well-spoken Mr Moy was in fact a representative of the Australian and/or the United States governments, despite his continued insistence that he was not. Moy received a letter from the leader of North Vietnam, Ho Chi Minh, inviting him to visit Hanoi to discuss the matter further. He set off across China for North Vietnam but was intercepted by young Red Guards who were at that time rampaging through the country, and was forced to return home. Moy next received from Ho Chi Minh an acceptance of his peace proposals, apart from a few minor alterations. At that stage Moy took the Department of Foreign Affairs in

Canberra into his confidence and informed their officials what he had been doing. Commonwealth policemen took Moy off his farm to a motel room in the nearby township of Ballina and questioned him even more closely than the Chinese had done. They confiscated whatever of his documents that they could lay their hands on, but had to turn him loose. Moy heard absolutely nothing further about the matter from either the Australian Government, the Chinese or the North Vietnamese. In disgust he abandoned his solo efforts in the international sphere. He sold his farm and prospered in business in Ballina where he became a wealthy and respected townsman.

The Australian government gradually lost political ground over the Vietnam War, even though it had won an election on the same issue. The government did its best but the people were becoming much more resistant to propaganda, especially the well-informed and increasingly critical younger people of Australia. Sir Robert Menzies had mercifully retired from politics, but the new generation began to see Harold Holt as being merely a later edition of Menzies. Other Australians seriously wondered why they had permitted themselves to become so enthusiastic about Holt at the time of the visit by President Johnson.

Australia, however, still produced some gallant fighting soldiers. Major Badcoe, for example, was able to send home to his wife in Canberra the U.S. Silver Star which he had been awarded for having rescued an American soldier under enemy fire in a village in South Vietnam early in 1967. Later he sent home to her two medals which had been given to him by the South Vietnam Government for gallantry. In April 1967, the major was killed in a grenade attack on a Viet Cong machine gun post. He was posthumously awarded the Victoria Cross, the British equivalent of the U.S. Congressional Medal of Honour. Australia did not have its own bravery medals to give to its own soldiers. Therefore all that the Australian Government could send to Major Badcoe's widow that was uniquely Australian was a letter of condolence from the Prime Minister.

People wanted to believe that the Vietnam War and the loss of soldiers like Major Badcoe had been worthwhile. There was no doubt that the war had delayed peasant revolutions in countries in South East Asia. There was every indication, however, that the governments which had been saved temporarily by the United States remained as isolated from their people as they had been at the beginning of the war and would eventually be overthrown. All that the delay had achieved had been to make millionaires of many of the corrupt officials in those governments through American aid, and sometimes with tacit American approval to keep on side. Some high-ranking government men in South East Asia, supposedly helping the U.S., made their own bankroll by becoming involved in peddling heroin and other hard drugs to American troops.

Australia's rewards from the Vietnam War were deservedly minute. Her small efforts earned more adverse criticism than praise, despite the deaths of more than 500 of her soldiers and the wounding of 2,000 more. The reaction of Americans to the Australian war effort ranged from the surprise of Senator Fulbright upon hearing of it to the stony indifference of the large bulk of the American population. Nor could it be said that Australia's defence capability had been much improved by the war involvement, or that her economy had received much of a boost. Most of Australia's war requirements had been purchased from other countries.

U.S. war contracts worth a total of $U.S.1,000 million were awarded to South Korea which had put 50,000 troops into South Vietnam, but the Australian government had been so ready to roll onto its back to please the United States that it had not had the nerve to press for war contracts.

It had been vitally in Australia's best interests that the United States should have remained strong and healthy and confident and outgoing. The Vietnam War had brought about exactly the opposite. American strength had been wasted and weakened, the nation's morale had been eroded, and her people sickened of the American role of international policeman. It would require the lapse of many years before the Americans would get over it. Australians, if they continued to lean heavily upon American protection, would need to pray for that time to pass in peace. Involvement in the Vietnam War exhibited America's incredibly bad judgement in international affairs — good intentions and folly, misguided persuasion and violence all mixed hopelessly from the outset. But Australia's involvement in the Vietnam War exhibited nothing more than a shabby willingness by the third-rate government of a second-rate nation to crawl to the United States Administration.

9

The Hollywood pioneers

To the majority of Australians the half a million square miles of country across the top of Australia is unknown. Mention of it sometimes stirs the sluggish imaginations of city dwellers in the south. They think of it as a distant place of spaciousness, primitive freedom and rugged adventure, but hardly a land in which to live with one's family. The tropical climate of the far north of Australia dissuades southern Australians from going there, just as the thought of the Arctic climate of Alaska deters urban-Americans from heading north. The Australian southern climate, however, has ferocious heat in summer almost as uncomfortable as the humidity of the tropics, and in the winter its wet, cold weather is far less pleasant than the warmth and sunshine of northern Australia. Most Australians do not know this.

One of Australia's foremost engineers, Sir William Hudson, once said that he believed that Australia would have become far more populous and more prosperous had the country's earliest settlements been established 1,500 miles further north. Hudson was particularly impressed by the settlement-potential of the delta land watered by the great rivers of the north. Two of these rivers, the Burdekin and the Fitzroy, have sufficient water to irrigate areas as large as the southern State of Victoria. Hudson was distressed that the waters of these northern rivers were continuing to pour to waste into the ocean and that the land which they drained was still sparsely populated and under-developed. Australians had been unwilling or unable to come to grips with it.

Now that much of northern Australia is owned by Americans, some Australians are taking a belated interest in it, but still do not really know much about the area. It surprises many of those who do visit there that much of northern and central Australia bears a striking resemblance to the American wild west as portrayed on the movies. It has the same flat-topped hills that Australian movie fans have come to know, and it has the same expanses of unfenced grassland and scrub and occasional clumps of boulders. Much of it is like Texas used to be.

The Australian north is swarming with wildlife – animals, birds and reptiles – to say nothing of the insects. On the open range are freely roaming wild horses, wild cattle, wild water buffalo, wild donkeys and wild camels. Around the rivers and the waterholes colonies of lean and vicious wild pigs can often be found. There are big red and grey kangaroos, emus as tall as a man, screaming green flocks of budgerigars and myriads of red-backed finches. Squadrons of kite hawks are always wheeling in the daylight skies, and at night their places are taken by travelling wild geese, strung out in long slowly flapping lines. On the inland plains there are countless rabbits, and sheep as red as the dust through which they forage, wild brush turkeys, and wild dogs.

The rainfall of the north of Australia is double the annual rainfall of the United Kingdom, but all of it falls during the few months of the monsoonal summer. The elephant grass grows almost visibly during the wet season until it is a green jungle seven feet tall. At the end of the wet summer it dries off rapidly, and bends in the winds until it becomes a brittle brown tangle waist high, ready for the fires which race through the countryside for hundreds of miles, baring the ground once more.

The cattle spreads of the north are gigantic. Some are as large as countries in Europe. What is not cattle leases is Crown Land or reserved for Aborigines. It is a land so vast that everything that breathes is dwarfed and insignificant. It is possible to climb a low hill and see all around you an apparently empty world extending out to the curve of the horizon in every direction. Often the only visible work of man is the thin black thread of the transcontinental road along which occasional motor vehicles crawl like moving specks.

On some of the more remote and smaller cattle properties they still work the tough way. I once saw black stockmen proving it by marking young bulls under conditions which would make a modern Texan blanch. They did it by securing each beast in the holding yard with a rope tied to the back axle of an old truck. When they started the truck slowly forward in low gear they pulled each struggling and bucking bull off its legs, dragging it bodily through the dust on its side until it was jammed up against the fence. Then a flurry of blacks descended upon it through the dust, wielding knife, branding iron, and clipper. When the beast was released and stood up trembling and bawling, it had the station brand black and smoking upon its hip, a piece clipped out of one of its ears, and the points cut off its horns. Down its hind legs the blood was streaming to the dust of the yard where its testicles lay like two big red eggs until the station dogs carried them away.

Shrewd Americans found the Australian Northern Territory after the war while they were adapting big business methods to food production. The immensity of the Northern Territory and the cheapness of land there lent unlimited scope to the American methods.

In postwar United States, the small family farms which had dominated American agriculture, faced extinction. Business corporations and syndicates had been swallowing the small family holdings. In 1951 the average size of a farm in America was 215 acres. Twenty years later it had doubled. Mechanization had provided the key to efficiency in farming, but mechanization was not economic unless the land-holding was large. Capital-intensive technology had replaced the brawn, guts and sweat of farmers and their hired help. Up to 100,000 steers could be fed on a prepared formula at regular intervals throughout the day at the flick of a switch. One man working only three hours a day could comfortably look after 40,000 broiler chickens. Combine harvesters could strip the cobs from rows of corn at a time, while in adjoining paddocks other machinery sprayed fertilizers or chemicals, swiftly and thoroughly. Instead of farmers using guesswork, computers were determining the correct combination and rotation of crops. Nothing was left to guesswork. By 1972 a farmer starting out on his own in the United States required heavy establishment capital to become soundly competitive.

In Australia the drift of population from rural districts to the cities had been following the similar population trend in the United States, but reconstruction and modernization of rural industries had been resisted and delayed. More often than not each of one hundred small farmers in a rural district had struggled to remain an independent little king in his own kingdom, helped by the unpaid labour of his wife and children. Because of the labour problem each small Australian farmer had invariably put himself into debt by buying tractors and harvesters and other expensive machinery which his farm could not afford. For much of each year such machinery was idle in barns while the farmer's earnings often were barely sufficient to cover the instalment repayments on the machinery after other expenses and taxation. Few Australian farmers ever pooled their resources to economize through collective machinery investment, or combined their resources to work adjoining lands together.

Upon the insistence of the Country Party the coalition government in Australia had paid struggling farmers all sorts of subsidies to keep them going. The direction in which many of the farmers had gone had been backwards. In some districts farmers had failed because of poor markets at home or abroad, and in others by a run of poor seasons – but all too often their farm was simply a business which was too small or inefficient to be profitable. By 1972 Australia's farmers, spread over 250,000 rural holdings, had a total and gross indebtedness to institutional lenders of $2,108 million. This did not include debts to hire purchase companies and to merchants and other large sums unpaid. Vast tracts of farming land had passed into the ownership of banks and lending institutions.

The way had been opened for big business corporations and well-heeled investors and speculators to take over rural land in southern Australia as they already had done in the north. Americans, faced with heavy costs in the U.S. found the depressed prices for good farm land in Australia irresistible. They moved in quietly through Australian-based investment companies to replace the defeated, embittered and often bankrupt Australian farmers who had retreated to the cities. In the big tough land of Australia only unlimited capital, expert business management and modern technology could make a lasting and profitable success of some rural industries and ensure the development of some areas.

Foremost among the big-business pioneers in Australia had been Art Linkletter, an American radio and television personality. He had become involved financially in the Northern Territory as early as 1957 when he had been one of an American syndicate which had tried to grow rice for the Asian market on the sub-coastal plains near Darwin. Their project had been a failure. Every summer for four years torrential monsoonal rains had flooded their young rice. Millions of wild geese – which shooters had failed to thin out – descended to devour their seed. Drought had followed the rains, and the rice fields had baked hard under a merciless sun. The syndicate had lost several million dollars.

Linkletter admitted only temporary defeat. He and other millionaire Americans, including Allen T. Chase, moved to Esperance in Western Australia and tried again. Calling themselves the Hollywood Pioneers they took up ownership of 1,885,000 acres of sandy plain, 400 miles from Perth. It was undulating country covered with stunted scrub, and overrun with kangaroos. People had believed it useless until Australian scientists had discovered that it could be made fertile through the addition to its soil of trace elements of zinc, copper, and cobalt. Once these trace elements were added, with the further application of superphosphate and urea, its production capability became magnificent. But it cost plenty.

Linkletter and the Hollywood Pioneers were bent on establishing an empire of livestock pastures, orchards, and vegetable gardens. Linkletter bought 20,000 acres of the syndicate's holdings, and spent $35 an acre in developing improved pastures. After a few years of steady if not spectacular consolidation, Allen Chase sold his interests to an impressive combination of American financiers, including the Chase Manhattan Bank, American Factors, J. H. Whitney and Company – thereby adding considerably to the business power base.

Ken and Helen Lunde of Seattle, Washington, typified the ordinary Americans influenced in 1967 through Linkletter's remarks about Australia. The Lundes understood Linkletter to say that Australia was a land of great opportunity for young people. Ken Lunde was 42, but he left his job as executive with Norby Marine Supplies and took his wife to Adelaide. Two years later he was assistant manager of the Glenelg Migrant Hostel, a receiving centre for migrants of all countries. He liked to say that his only regret was that he had not gone to Australia earlier. He found life a lot easier. Linkletter became Australia's unofficial publicity officer in the U.S. through his frequent comments on radio and television – although not all American migrants became as satisfied as the Lundes.

Linkletter made a different sort of impact when he talked straight business. He revealed that he and his friends had been netting a return of about 15.6 per cent annually on their capital invested in Australia. After ten years their land had appreciated in value from about 50 cents an acre to around $15. Paved roads, telephones, schools, and a small shopping centre had come to their Australian empire, and so had plush neighbours like David Rockefeller.

Linkletter revealed that he had put money into other Australian ventures, together with Allen Chase, Jack Wrather, Albert E. Schwabacher and his brother Jack, Earl Slick of Texas, and John Brown Cook of Connecticut – all names known and respected in sound financial circles in the U.S. Linkletter listed his investments. He had a piece of the action in Fitzroy Station in the Northern Territory, which covered 750,000 acres with a big river running through it, and which was carrying several thousand cattle. He was in on a million-acre cattle station called Dunham near the Ord River cotton-growing area, and which was running 9,000 cattle. He had also been a purchaser of yet another million-acre property called Anna Plains which had 21,000 cattle and extensive experimental plantings of sorghum for the Japanese market. Linkletter claimed that his syndicate could supply a substantial part of the growing world demand for meat cheaper than any other cattle-growing district on Earth He pointed out that it cost about $25 a head to raise and market cattle in Australia which was about one third the cost in the United States. Most important of all, there was plenty of range and a new sympathetic tax structure for investment. Capital expenditures could be written off in five years up to 120 per cent of the cost. There was also a seven year loss-carry-forward available.

American ranchers were amazed when Linkletter told them that they could acquire properties of one million to four million acres for relatively little money. They gasped when he informed them that King Ranch of Texas had taken over 4,700 square miles of Australia on an annual lease agreement of $1.12 per square mile. Linkletter told Americans of Kaiser Steel who were digging out 15,000 million tons of iron ore from mineral leases near one of his cattle properties, and of the more recent finds in Australia of oil and gas, nickel, phosphate and bauxite. He also mentioned that the American cotton farmers in New South Wales had been guaranteed 40 cents a pound for their cotton for the next five years with unlimited acreage allowed. That price was seven cents a pound higher than the current Californian cotton price.

The easy pace of life in Australia was irritating for Linkletter, the go-getter tycoon. He warned his fellow

Americans about it, evidently not understanding that what he was complaining about would sound pretty good to the average hard-pressed American wage-earner caught up in the daily rat race. Linkletter put it this way: 'Many Americans who go there have trouble realizing that the pace in Australia is comparatively slow; things seldom get done in a hurry. A few disenchanted American families turn around and go home after only a short stay. Some dislike the way of life that appeals to Australian men – beer, gambling, going to horse races and working at just one pace – slow.' According to Linkletter Australians made no secret of their dislike of people who pushed and worked too hard and who were too obviously obsessed with striving for success and status. As a final hint to fellow Americans back in 1967 Linkletter told them that if they wished to become migrants to Australia despite all his warnings the Australian Government would pay $160 towards the cost of $560 for the air fare from California.

Henry Clark, a salesman of Pomona, Greater Los Angeles, spent every cent of his savings to migrate with his wife and four children 'to escape the business rat race'. He tried oyster farming – it being one of the most peaceful jobs he could think of. But at the age of 38 he went back into business as the Australian national marketing manager of the Minnesota Mining and Manufacturing Company. He said apologetically when he was appointed 'It would appear that I'm on the same treadmill again, but it's not the same in Australia. Business here is not pressure-cooked like it is in the States. People have time for people and are more courteous and honest.'

This book will give more space later to emigration from the U.S. to Australia but some instances have been mentioned in this chapter because of the Linkletter influence in 1967 on Americans who had become disenchanted with their own country. He was a pathfinder pointing the way to a new land and a fresh start. The Australian government wanted migrants from the U.S. and should have given Linkletter a reward. However, Art

Linkletter did well enough out of Australia – primarily through his pioneering courage.

One of Linkletter's Australian counterparts, Sir William Gunn, was in there pitching all the time for more American investment capital for Australian rural industries. In 1967, Gunn was 53, six feet two inches tall and weighing 245 pounds. He had a disconcerting habit of glowering from beneath his low hair line, and he parted his hair dead in the middle. Gunn had become the managing director of Gunn Rural Management which managed sixteen properties in the Northern Territory and Queensland, totalling 17,000 square miles and running 110,000 cattle. Gunn enthused: 'I see Australia as another United States. I see it as the equivalent of the United States of the 1830s when they had only about 11 million people – but our future is brighter. Look at the technology advances since then, and think of what will happen in the next century. I'm glad I'm in food because I see Australia as a great food bowl – and food will be our best ammunition with the world population possibly doubling within the next thirty-three years.'

It was interesting how almost everyone in Australia still related almost every Australian industry to the defence of the country. When Sir William Gunn confused food with ammunition he was doing no more than revealing himself to be a typical Australian fearful of his country's defencelessness and always ready to pay lip-service to the need to do something about it. The nation had the perpetual unease of feeling surrounded by potential enemies, and the perpetual guilt of being too lazy to do much about it. Lip-service to defence was always sure of a popular reception in Australia and was useful in helping to establish any new business enterprise.

The optimistic Gunn was proud of being a fourth generation Australian. His great grandfather had migrated from Scotland in 1861 to go onto the land. It was Sir William's boast that he had become so independent that no one could buy 100 per cent of his time and that he could do almost anything he pleased. His self-confidence often resembled that of the loud and expansive Texans with whom he did business. Australians resented Gunn's efforts to sell off large chunks of northern Australia to the Americans.

Gunn had long since become discouraged from hawking his business ideas around Australia in the hope of raising the money he required to put them into practice. Consequently he now headed for New York every time he needed extra finance instead of trying to obtain it in Sydney or Melbourne. In October 1971 Gunn quietly went to the United States to raise $7 million for his new company, Gunn Resources and Exploration Incorporated, which had massive land holdings in the Northern Territory and Queensland. He issued a prospectus in America inviting participation of equity capital in five great cattle spreads with a combined acreage slightly larger than Spain. A team of 700 salesmen went to work selling initial stock options at $7 a share. The Americans snapped them up as a gift.

The thing about it that really stung the Australians was that they did not hear about Gunn's land sale until after he had reached the United States. They further learned with considerable pain that the prospectus for investment in Gunn's company could not be issued in their own country because it did not comply with the Australian Companies Act. The prospectus had been specifically designed to meet the requirements of the American Securities and Exchange Commission. This meant that any Australians wishing to buy shares in the company had to make arrangements in the United States to do it. Overnight Sir William Gunn became as popular in Australia as an Arab in Israel. A Labor member of the Queensland Parliament, Mr Aiken, declared that he had been shocked and horrified that shares of Queensland land were being sold in the United States at 'a lousy $7 a share'. Mr Aiken said it made the peaceful invasion and foreign ownership of vast areas of Australia a distinct possibility and that such careless disregard for Australian ownership was nothing less than criminal and traitorous.

So politically emotive was the outcry that the Acting Prime Minister of the time, Douglas Anthony, arranged for exchange control approval so that Australians could invest in the company. This did not appease the Labor Party. The Leader of the Federal Opposition asked the Government to consider the fact that Sir William Gunn was a member of the Board of the Reserve Bank and therefore would sit in judgement on applications for shares in the company. It was the Reserve Bank which had administered guidelines on overseas investment in Australia since 1965.

When Sir William Gunn returned to Australia he stood at bay in the VIP lounge at the airport terminal confronted by a pack of journalists eager to bring him down. Sir William's big frame had become thick and bloat-bellied from insufficient exercise combined with a hearty appetite. His pudgy face was pale from the fatigue of long working hours and insufficient rest and his eyes were bloodshot. He lowered his head to think before answering each question and the part down the centre of his thick black brilliantined hair was like the scar of a knife wound. But Sir William was neither shamefaced nor apologetic for what he had been doing in America. He explained in his rumbling way that he had tried to get the money he needed in Australia before going to the U.S. but had failed. He pointed out that his company previously had been the Gunn Land and Exploration Partnership with capital of $4.5 million of which only $800,000 was Australian money. Gunn said that in his prospectus for his latest project he had warned Americans that it would be a long term investment before profits, and involved a high risk factor. Australians were just not willing to provide money for that sort of business venture. They wanted quick returns. So he had turned to the Americans.

The public furore over the Gunn episode and over similar sales of Australian land was partly reflective of the lack of public confidence in their own government. Australians generally believed that American businessmen and the U.S. Government could outwit their leaders in

Canberra with the utmost ease. The Australian public therefore was chronically apprehensive that every new business activity involving Americans in Australia had an element of robbery in it somewhere which their Canberra guardians were too stupid to detect.

The newspapers continued to carry stories about the extension of U.S. cattlemen's interest in Australia. Land in Australia in 1972 with the same carrying capacity as that in American cattle country was available for $70 to $100 an acre, compared with $500 to $600 an acre for similar U.S. properties. Australian land prices had been climbing steeply since the Hollywood Pioneers had first bought some of it, but Americans continued to find the prices cheap. Among the late-comers forming a new buying syndicate were 100 members of the Montana Cattlemen's Association.

In the Kimberley district in the Australian West meatworks had been built to slaughter range-fed cattle for the U.S. hamburger trade. An American-owned group, the Australian Land and Cattle Company, was going ahead with plans to spend $A18 million on a pioneering irrigation scheme for farming and beef-raising on the Fitzroy River. The Americans of this company had a plan for a vertically integrated and diversified farming and ranching enterprise of five divisions with immediate earnings from their cattle holdings. The scheme was worth looking at in some detail because of its magnitude and international ramifications, and because it provided an excellent example of the manner in which American business methods could organize farming to tame a wilderness and make a profit. The first division was the Kimberley cattle division which was to supply the United States market for boneless beef and which would also provide young steers for fattening in the second division. The second division, the Inkata feed yard division, would supply the Japanese market for prime beef. The third division, the Camballin Irrigation Farm Division, would export grain sorghum to Japan and supply stockfeed for the second division. The fourth division would take care of machinery supply requirements for the entire scheme. It had bought out major machinery agents supplying the West Kimberley district with motor vehicles and tractors and other necessary equipment, and would wholesale these goods to the scheme. The fifth division was the Marketing Division based in the city of Perth. Its purpose was to scout the world to locate new markets for the scheme's products. The Marketing Division formed an alliance with the Japanese trading house of C. Itoh and Company which was investing at least one million dollars in the project. This partnership gave the scheme a permanent bridgehead into other parts of South East Asia. The American principals and their Japanese associates saw it as a food supplier which would eventually market its products among 2,000 million Asians living within a 5,000 miles arc to the north.

In 1971, another group of Americans, Goddard of Australia Pty Limited, began building a dam on the Dunham River to supply water for dry-season irrigation of fodder for cattle-raising and to produce grain crops with an export potential. Other American and Australian businessmen had been injecting large amounts of money into the open range cattle industry of the Kimberleys and in other parts of Western Australia and the Northern Territory. They had been upgrading herds with fresh bloodstock and had been fencing and improving pastures and watering places.

American mining interests had also begun diversifying their investments by going into the western cattle business. One of these had been Amax which had purchased the huge Mitchell River cattle station adjoining its bauxite holdings and which planned to improve the size and quality of its herds. Amax had joined the business-pastoral giants of Australia. It was using international finance and international marketing in the best American tradition. Also in the American style it was holding enormous areas of Australia which would appreciate in value in the future. Not so commendable were the American speculators who had been buying Australian land and holding it for appreciation and resale without spending a cent on its development. By 1972 these absentee American owners were getting a bad reputation and some of it was rubbing off unfairly on U.S. developers. Northern Australia and the west are still wide open, but conditions have been changing. Communications have become better and faster. The Australian government has spent $25 million over ten years improving 1,600 miles of roads – a small investment but helpful. The greatest changes are being made by American money and methods.

Part of the modernization in northern Australia has included the capture and domestication of many of the 200,000 buffaloes which had been roaming wild. Buffaloes cost about $14 each to domesticate. The buffalo-hunters lasso them from four-wheel drive vehicles and drag them off their feet. The hunters receive their instructions from scouts and messengers riding motor cycles across the plains. Most of the buffalo-hunters are Australians – but Americans, such as those on the W. R. Grace property at Mount Bundy, have been involved also.

As the buffalo herds are improved and built up they are put on the same grazing paddocks as cattle. The buffaloes clear away the long and ranker native grasses following the wet season, thus permitting improved pastures to grow for the cattle. Mount Bundy Station set a beef target early in 1971 for a population of 60,000 cattle, running with 15,000 buffaloes. Buffalo meat could not be distinguished from beef in southern shops. It was lean meat, excellent for the U.S. market.

The great bargain sale of Australian land to Americans which began with the purchases by the Hollywood Pioneers is continuing. Some northern and western regions of Australia almost seem to have become provinces of the United States. They are areas of American accents, American manners and working methods, American women and kids, American quarter horses and lariats and white sombreros. They have become areas of American determination to stay put and build an economic stronghold in Australia.

Stories in newspapers every week continue to recount the American grab of cheap Australian land, American development projects in Australia, American expansion in Australia. It is a galling experience for Australians who are suddenly coming up with schemes of their own but who complain that they are being thwarted by not having sufficient capital to match American bidding. Popular sentiment in Australia dubiously prefers American ownership to most other foreign ownership, but the general feeling remains that of the householder who resents outsiders coming in and digging up his backyard. Even friends and relatives have no right to do that . . . And there remains also the public's distrust in the men of government in Canberra. Is Canberra ever going to do anything about the Americans?

In the *Australian* newspaper of 18 September 1971 was the following front page story: 'Americans are negotiating to buy 1,024,000 acres of the Simpson Desert, near the Queensland-Northern Territory border, at a price of 20 cents an acre.' The newspaper explained that the U.S. purchasers were operating through the Overseas Real Estate Trust, based in Hong Kong. Cattlemen who had recently taken a look at the Simpson Desert had reported that it was covered with grass and wildflowers after recent rains, and carried good feed for cattle for at least two years.

Australians felt angry about it. When Americans started buying up their deserts – and through companies in Hong Kong – and at 20 cents an acre – it was getting close to the bottom of the barrel. It was too much like the last pieces of Australia being offered in Asian street markets.

In Federal Parliament, Dr D. Everingham, Labor, announced that he wished to offer a higher bid of 25 cents for one acre of the Simpson Desert. Later Dr Everingham urged all Australians to write to the Minister for the Interior with cash offers for government land to prevent it from falling into foreign ownership. This mischievous appeal received an astounding response. Every day hundreds of cash donations poured into Canberra to buy one acre blocks of the Simpson Desert. Individual contributions ranged from 25 cents to $10 but there were some written promises for amounts of up to $1,000. Large Australian business companies might not be prepared to risk money outside the capital cities, but the little people of Australia, the wage-earning public, were demonstrating how they felt about it. The Minister for the Interior found difficulty in speaking civilly to Dr Everingham. He was forced to deny strongly in the parliament that the government was putting the Simpson Desert up for sale. He explained that evidently there had been a loose journalistic description of the land for sale through the Overseas Real Estate Trust. Possibly some of the land was close to the Simpson Desert, but it was not part of the government-owned desert. Despite the Minister's denial the public money continued to be posted to Canberra. The government had to employ a special task force of clerks to post it back again. Someone unkindly worked out that it was costing the government 65 cents to return each of the 25 cent bids. The matter did not end there. Dr Everingham and some of his Labor associates announced that in all seriousness they were setting up a people's land-buying organization. They were going to call it the Australian Heritage Company. It would offer 25 cent shares to thousands of Australians until eventually the company had sufficient money to buy one million acres of land somewhere on the Australian continent. This land would be saved from foreign ownership and would become in perpetuity an Australian park and nature reserve ... The public applauded the idea. It would be an Australian enclave within Australia.

On 21 March 1972, a Labor Member of Parliament, Al Grassby lamented: 'Here's a new figure. Overseas corporations now own 250 million acres while dispossessed Australians are streaming off the land.'

10

Americans in mining

The collapse of the market for wool in the late 1960s and early 1970s would have been crippling had not new income been discovered. Beneath the parched soil of inland Australia over which the merino sheep had snuffled in their search for herbage was new treasure, far exceeding wool in value. American geologists and American money played a leading part in finding it.

The earliest and best example of American expertise and dogged determination, backed by money, had been the success of the Mount Isa mine in western Queensland. A small company Mount Isa Mines Limited, had been working during the 1930s to extract lead, silver and zinc from beneath the bare red earth and rocks of the desert. Twice up to 1939 the company had been saved from insolvency by the American Smelting and Refining Company, and had third mortgage debentures underwritten by the Pearl Assurance Company of London.

One of the central figures in the story of persistent work and courage at Mount Isa was an American mining engineer, Julius Kruttschnitt, who had become general manager of Mount Isa Mines Limited late in 1930, and Chairman of Directors in 1937. Kruttschnitt was mainly responsible for keeping the mine going through its poor years, never losing hope that things would improve. His faith was rewarded when massive lodes of copper were located.

By 1953 Mount Isa had become the world's richest copper mine and its future was assured. Kruttschnitt retired, stating that the time had come for a younger man to take over his job. Thirteen years later the reserves of copper ore at Mount Isa had been proven up to 41.5

million tons, with grades of up to 3.8 per cent. Since then larger reserves have been located.

The late chief of the Commonwealth Bureau of Mineral Resources in Canberra, Sir Harold Raggatt, had a lasting admiration for Kruttschnitt. In his book, *Mountains of Ore*, published in 1968, Raggatt paid him the supreme compliment by describing him as 'as good an Australian as any native-born Australian I have ever known.'

Another American, Lewis G. Weeks, a highly experienced petroleum geologist, was responsible for the discovery of major oil and gas fields off the southern coast of Victoria. In March 1969, Australian Iron and Steel Limited, a subsidiary of BHP Proprietary Company Limited, hired Weeks to advise them on exploration prospects. Weeks counselled against further exploration in the Sydney Basin in which the company had been interested. He recommended that an exploration acreage be taken up off the Gippsland coast of Victoria. At that time offshore technology was in its infancy, having been in practice only five to ten years. Weeks, however, insisted that it would develop to the stage where economic recovery of oil and natural gas would be possible over any continental shelf to depths of 50 fathoms.

The Gippsland Basin was extensively surveyed. The results of the surveys indicated that Weeks had probably been right on target with the advice he had given. In May 1964 the Australian company reached an agreement to take as an operating partner, Esso Exploration and Production Australia Incorporated – a subsidiary of Standard Oil (New Jersey). A ship-shaped drilling unit, *Glomar 111*, owned by Global Marine Incorporated, was taken on contract for two years for a wildcat drilling programme destined to prove successful. The vessel sailed from Houston, Texas, in October 1964, and arrived on site in December.

The first well, Barracouta A1 blew out on 18 February next year. After it was controlled it flowed gas and condensate at rates up to 9.6 million cubic feet a day. Other gas and oil strikes were made quickly in the same locality.

On the west coast of Australia Sir William Walkley had much more trouble in making an oil strike. He needed $A60 million – not much in the international oil industry, but too much for risk money in Australia. He hawked his exploration scheme around London but had to return home to report to his directors that the British were as interested as if he had suggested that they should help him hunt seals in the desert at Alice Springs. He had to go to Los Angeles to get the money. His first support in Los Angeles came from the Richfield Corporation but they later pulled out through fear that an Australian Labor Government would nationalize any oil or gas discovery made. However, Standard Oil of California and the Texas Company entered into a joint venture with the Australians and formed a company with them known as West Australian Petroleum Proprietary Limited. Together they went on to discover the Barrow Island oil field and the Dongara gas fields north of Perth, bringing a new industrial potential to the previously forlorn west of the Australian continent.

In 1957 a South Australian company, Santos Limited, had sought the help of the Delhi-Taylor Oil Corporation to provide necessary technical and financial resources in its search for oil and gas. The American company made a thorough investigation before committing itself. It considered the attitude of the Australian government and the various State governments of Australia toward foreign investment, the demand for petroleum products within Australia, the rate of growth of this demand, the political stability of the Australian government, and general economic conditions within Australia. Fortunately for everyone concerned Australia passed the test. In May 1958 the Americans reached an agreement with Santos to earn a 50 per cent interest in the Santos holdings, and under which the Americans were required to spend $2,500,000 in exploratory operations. Late in 1962 the expenditure obligation was fulfilled and Santos became a full paying partner under a new agreement. On 31 December 1963, drilling at Gidgealpa, not far from the border intersections of South Australia, Queensland and New South Wales, established the presence of a gasfield of major proportions. The Gidgealpa gas field was later to supply natural gas to Sydney and surrounding industrial centres on the east coast.

American capital and mining skill joined Australian initiative and British capital in developing one of the greatest iron ore discoveries in the world in Western Australia. In fact, one of the largest bodies of ore was named Mount Tom Price in honour of the late Vice President of the Kaiser Steel Corporation. Price made the following comment after his first visit to the area. 'There are mountains of iron ore there. It is just staggering. It is like trying to calculate how much air there is.'

The man who made the find was Lang Hancock, small-time miner, and owner of local cattle stations, Mulga Downs and Hamersley. Hancock, a man as barrel-shaped as his own prime beef bulls and sometimes as aggressive, made the find while flying south with his wife for their Christmas holidays in 1952. They had been crossing the Hamersley Ranges in their light aircraft when storm clouds closed in and forced them down to lower altitudes. Hancock decided that the best way through the Hamersley Ranges would be to follow the course of the Turner River at tree top level. In his own words: 'The river went through a deep gorge. Its sheer walls were 200 feet high. They appeared to be iron. This was the first time I had been close to this inaccessible country, though I had flown over it frequently at much greater altitude ... The cliffs of the gorge absorbed my interest so much that I resolved to return in good weather and examine them more closely. I returned in April and began an aerial survey, finding a place to land. I took samples, made quantity estimates, and realized that this was a major discovery ...'

Any person who could fly at tree top level following a river course through a gorge in inaccessible ranges in bad weather and still find time to make a mineral discovery by becoming absorbed in the passing walls of rock near his wing tips just had to be a remarkable man. Perhaps too little has been said in praise of the nerve of his passenger, Mrs Hancock.

At first Hancock could not do anything about his iron ore discovery. Since 1938 it had been government policy to prohibit the exporting of iron ore to conserve existing known reserves for home use. The embargo had helped to stop any large scale search for iron ore in Australia, but the position was worse in Western Australia where all deposits were reserved to the Crown and were not available for pegging by individuals or companies.

For years geologists had been insisting that the original estimates of Australia's iron ore reserves were nonsense, and in 1960 they prevailed upon the Commonwealth government to partially lift the export embargo. This was followed in 1961 by the Western Australian government introducing reforms permitting the granting of titles for the prospecting for and the development of iron deposits. And when that happened Lang Hancock drew out the ace which he had been keeping up his sleeve for almost ten years. He revealed the existence of the Pilbara iron ore deposits which he had found in 1952.

In December 1962 geologists estimated the reserves of iron ore at Pilbara at not less than 380 million tons of ore containing 60/61 per cent iron. Soon afterwards these reserves were enlarged to 4,860 million tons of ore of over 50 per cent iron. An estimate of their money value later was $A38,880 million.

Hamersley Holdings Pty Limited and Hamersley Iron Pty Limited were formed with 60 per cent of both companies owned by a British subsidiary, Conzinc Riotinto of Australia Pty Limited and 40 per cent by Kaiser Steel Corporation of California. In March 1967, in deference to a public outcry, 10 per cent of the equity was offered to the Australian public in the form of ten million fifty cent shares in Hamersley Holdings. It was a little taste of honey to shut them up.

Hancock, whose part in forming the two mining companies was described by one Australian newspaper as 'his brute force drive and restless energy', was not left behind the door when cash benefits were paid out from his ore discovery. He and his partner, Peter Wright settled for 2½ per cent royalties in Hamersley Iron, and Hancock's income rose to $30,000 a day. But by 1971 he had bigger plans for developing new ore leases and for building steelworks from which he could reasonably expect to earn twice that much. Art Linkletter had been somewhat astray in his assertion that people could not get rich quickly in Australia.

Hancock's philosophy was that of the self-made man. He told a newspaper reporter, 'I believe, bad and all as it is, that the greed of capitalism is the only driving force there is.'

In the wake of Hancock other iron ore projects on equally as vast a scale were developed in Western Australia, but Hancock's companies continued to attract the most attention because they had been first in the field. Under their agreement with the Western Australian State Government they had to spend $77 million over thirty years. By the time the first shipment of ore was made in August 1966 expenditure had exceeded $108 million – and the completed project of mine, railway tracks connecting the ore body to a new port at Dampier 182 miles away and the new port itself had meant a further payout of $52 million. This was development capital which would have been beyond the ability of Australians to provide without international assistance. A town had been constructed at the mining site and another at the shipping port where wharves and facilities had to be built for ore carriers of over 100,000 tons. It was all done by the Australians working on the project well within the scheduled time, despite claims that the undertaking would fail because of the remoteness of the area and the sweltering climate. It was a remarkable achievement.

When I flew over Mount Tom Price in 1970 it had become difficult to believe that it had all happened so quickly. The iron mountain in the wilderness had been terraced. Gigantic trucks were being loaded by even bigger mechanical grabs. The ore was being transferred to the railhead and onto waiting rail trucks at rapid speed. In the nearby township every house was air-conditioned. There were smooth green lawns and flower gardens and well stocked stores, a pub surrounded by a white stone wall to shelter it from the desert wind, and an olympic swimming pool which resembled a blue jewel from the air. The town was a patch of civilization in a harsh red country through which were thrusting the bare red ribs of the naked iron ore deposits.

The second of the three largest of the iron ore developers in Western Australia was a wholly-owned subsidiary of American Metal Climax, Mount Newman Iron Ore Company Limited. It had entered into an agreement with the Western Australian government for the mining of ore reserves in a huge new find in the Ophthalmia Range. It assigned its rights and obligations to a consortium of various other companies including American, Australian and Japanese holdings, and began operating to a new port at Port Hedland, connected by a new railtrack 265 miles long. It was almost a duplicate of the Mount Tom Price project.

Early in 1961, Cyprus Mines Corporation of Los Angeles, and Utah Construction and Mining Company of San Francisco with Consolidated Goldfields (Australia) Pty Limited, became equal partners in the Mount Goldsworthy mine, 70 miles east of Port Hedland. In January 1965, this group signed a contract with Japanese steel mills providing for the export of $16\frac{1}{2}$ million tons of ore between 1966 and 1972. Similar towns, railway tracks and port facilities had to be constructed as for the other two mines.

A further giant iron ore project being started at Mount Eden at the head of the Robe River was in Australian hands but seemed likely to wind up under American and Japanese control due to the insolvency of the Australian company.

By 1971 the three main company consortiums involved

in the Western Australian iron ore province – the Hamersley, Mount Newman, and Goldsworthy groups – had invested $A1,000 million in production facilities and infrastructure, but it was estimated that by 1975 their iron exports from Western Australia would be worth $600 million annually. Their future profits seemed so gigantic that Australians gnashed their teeth in impotent rage. But the development cost of the iron ore industry in Western Australia had been quite beyond Australia's financial resources. Had international money not been used up to the end of 1971 the development of the iron ore reserves on the current scale would have required a contribution of $80 from every man, woman and child in the Australian nation.

The iron ore province of Western Australia was in a part of the continent which once had been condemned as useless. It was an area of 90,000 square miles within the tropics but at altitudes of up to 4,000 feet above sea level. The average annual rainfall was only about ten inches and in summer many successive days of 100-degree temperatures were common. The winter climate was pleasant with a temperature range between 50 and 75 degrees. Local water supplies from underground bores were plentiful, except on the coast where the need for de-salination plants had to be considered. Before the iron ore had been found most of the area had been uninhabited, except for a few cattle stations and a few tiny settlements along the coast.

In July 1971, the Australian Minister for National Development, Mr Swartz, put Australia's iron ore reserves at 20,000 million tons. As well as being one of the largest deposits in the world they were among the richest. Millions of tons of the ore assayed at around 62 per cent iron. Deposits of 56 per cent or slightly less were regarded as low grade. Visiting American miners accustomed to working much lower grades in the United States were excited by the value of the Western Australian finds. One group of Americans visiting Mount Tom Price became so interested in the road upon which their bus was travelling that they made a closer examination of the surface material. After having made a few inquiries one of them exclaimed to a friend: 'My God, Elmer! This road assays 52 per cent!'

The Australian public, prompted by a nagging press, grew restive about exports of iron ore to foreign steelworks. It was popularly agreed that more steelworks should be built on Australian soil to use iron ore from Western Australia, and that Australia should aim to be an exporter of steel and other finished products rather than be supplying raw materials indefinitely to the industries of foreign countries. The theory was splendid, but the cost prohibitive. It was estimated, for a starter that an expenditure of around $3,000 million would be required to establish one large new steelworks on the west coast of Australia and another on the east coast. Raising such great amounts of investment capital in a country of Australia's size would have been somewhat like a canary trying to lay a duck's egg.

Therefore it came down once more to the need for foreign capital investment if Australia was to have additional steelworks. Australians did not like the idea – but most seemed to agree, judging from the tone of the Australian press, that it would be preferable to have foreign-owned steelworks in Australia and using local ore to exporting all of the ore to foreign-owned steelworks overseas. Australians grumbled that the profits from such investments would probably go to the United States, but at least the new steelworks would be providing more jobs in Australia and would be giving greater depth to Australian industrialization.

The American companies in the Mount Newman consortium, the American Armco Group, and the Australian company BHP were in fact making a close study of the feasibility of building new steelworks in Australia. They were concerned about heading off the increasing domination of world steel markets by the Japanese mills which had been expanding fast with the benefit of cheap iron ore from Australia.

In July 1971 these investigations gained new interest when a British-Australian partnership, Woodside-Burmah, made the first of a series of colossal discoveries of natural gas on the continental shelf only 80 miles from the western iron ore port of Dampier. Subsequent strikes rapidly outlined the gas field as one of the world's largest, both in area and in reserves. These finds suddenly had added dramatic new possibilities to the industrialization of Western Australia. The convenient and cheap new power source available promised to enable steel mills in Western Australia to outproduce and undersell any other steelmakers in Asia, America or Europe – given adequate time and development money.

There again was the stone over which Australian nationalists stumbled. Australia simply did not have the kind of development money needed. Therefore the combination of new steelworks, gas field and iron ore deposits simply added up to greater new opportunities for the rich American and British corporations. The Australians were virtually becoming spectators of a game on their home ground and for which even the entrance fee was more than they could afford.

The early years of the 1970s had become an era in which startling things were happening all over the Australian continent due largely to American money and technology. It had become evident that Australia would be a leading nation in mineral production for many years into the future. In addition to iron ore, nickel and copper, there were immense deposits of coal, and staggering new finds of uranium. Much of the northern coastal country of Cape York Peninsula was found to have a top layer of red bauxite pebbles, and it represented cream on top of the cake for the alumina industry.

Companies caught up by the forced pace of the Australian mineral discoveries were compelled by economic necessity to adopt an international outlook, not only to marketing but to production. A good example of the need for an international operation because of controlling circumstances occurred in the mining of the Cape York bauxite. The owners of the lease, the Australian-based British company, Consolidated Zinc Corporation Limited, needed partners to raise the huge amount of development capital required and to provide experience in the production of alumina or aluminum. But the company also had to solve another problem. A large part of the non-Communist world's aluminum industry was controlled by five existing international groups, Alcoa, Reynolds, and Kaiser in the United States, Alcan in Canada, and Pechinery in Europe. Therefore, there was virtually no free market in aluminum and the free market for alumina was small. Consolidated Zinc Corporation Limited decided that if it could not beat them it would have to join them. It took in as partners Kaiser Aluminum and Chemical Corporation, and then faded out of sight through another company merger which produced a strong new organization, Conzinc Riotinto of Australia Limited. The international consortium took on yet another identity, Comalco Industries Pty Limited. When the stirring of the pot had been completed the Australian share inside the mixture worked out at exactly 17.38 per cent.

Comalco spawned a second new consortium company, Queensland Alumina Limited to build and operate an alumina plant at Gladstone on the east coast of Queensland. Its only function was to produce alumina for its owners who agreed to take the following percentages of the product: Kaiser 44 per cent, Alcan 20 per cent, Pechinery 20 per cent and Comalco 16 per cent. Comalco owned only 8 per cent of Queensland Alumina Limited but Australians could at least say that 17.38 per cent of that 8 per cent was Australian-owned.

The Gladstone alumina plant was designed to have an output of 600,000 tons of alumina and was the largest installation built anywhere in the world. Its cost was $104 million. Production began in March 1967, and three months later the first shipment of alumina left Gladstone for Intalco in the United States. By May 1967 the capacity of the plant had been increased to

900,000 tons. Up on Cape York Peninsula 2½ million tons of bauxite pebbles were being mined and shipped out each year.

11
Banana Republic

Prime Minister Gorton was frequently accused of trying to run his government like an American president. Gorton thought he understood the American mind and methods, particularly in matters of defence. It was odd that with his American tendencies he also gained the reputation of being the most refreshingly Australian prime minister that Australia ever had.

Gorton's own wife, Bettina, was an American citizen, who had been born in Bangor in the State of Maine. She was intelligent and strong-principled and Gorton often listened closely to her opinions. They were an Australian-American team in themselves, but as leaders in a country like Australia they faced severe problems.

As in a banana republic almost everything touching on defence in Australia had something of the fraudulent or the farcical. Conscription for the Vietnam War had given Australia a small but well-trained army reserve, but the army lacked sufficient weapons and equipment to be expanded quickly into an effective force to protect the Australian mainland. The Navy's flagship was a superannuated British carrier which had sunk one Australian and one American destroyer in two sea collisions, both of them resulting in heavy loss of Australian and American lives. The Navy's most powerful ships were three modern destroyers which had been built in American shipyards. The Australian government had not believed that its own aircraft industry could build replacement aircraft to modernize the ageing Australian Air Force, but had spent $300 million in buying experimental F111 bombers from the United States ten years before they were fit to be flown, and there were only twenty-four of them.

At the ceremonials frequently held in Australian cities the saluting areas were always thick with bemedalled Australian generals and admirals and air vice marshalls. The younger people looking curiously at them were apt to laugh aloud and wonder what they all commanded. Australia had an army general for every company of its few battalions, an admiral for each of its ships, and enough senior air force officers to pilot a couple of squadrons.

One of Australia's most experienced diplomats, Mr W. R. Crocker disclosed the depth of his disgust for Australian defence policy-linked-with-politics when he became free to speak after his retirement in 1971. He claimed that fear was a major ingredient of the foreign policy of Australia and that this was bred from ignorance and that both spread into Australia's defence attitudes. He said that as a result of ignorance Australia had been prone to a satellism to the United States of a singularly passive and uncritical sort. Australians had accepted American public estimates and attitudes on virtually all the great issues of the past two decades.

Crocker said that Australians had made speeches at the United Nations, and diplomatic representations in various world capitals, at American request and at times in the very phrases concocted by the American Administration in Washington. He added that the assiduity and docility of Australia in this respect had been paralleled only by Russia's tamest, or most cowed satellites. He said that the role of sycophant to America or to anyone else was not natural to the Australian character and was both unnecessary and dangerous.

Crocker placed much of the blame for Australia's diplomatic subservience upon Federal politicians whom he described as being frequently ignorant of the outside world or lacking in curiosity about it. He claimed that Australian cabinet ministers tended not to want expert advice, and least of all if it ran counter to their own political slogans or political attitudes. Writing in the quarterly magazine, *Review* published by the Institute of Public Affairs, Crocker stressed the falsity of one of the political-defence catch-cries issuing from Canberra over a long stretch of years. 'The threat from China' had become as familiar in Australia as the slogan 'there is no substitute for wool' – but the Australian Department of Foreign Affairs did not have one person specializing on China. Evidently the information it used was provided from the United States.

The people of Western Australia who had always felt separated from the rest of the nation would have felt more secure had an American fleet moved into the Indian Ocean and used ports along the west coast of Australia as permanent bases. After Vietnam, however, Washington was concerned with finding ways of reducing its defence expenditure, not increasing it. A competition against Russia for command of the Indian Ocean had no immediate appeal to the U.S.

Nevertheless, on the night of 14 August 1969 the Australian Minister for External Affairs, Gordon Freeth, startled his Parliament by stating that the Australian Government was looking forward to co-operation with Russia for Asian regional security and development. He said that Australia and the Soviet Union had already begun talks involving bilateral relations and wider issues. Furthermore, Freeth toned down in his speech the future likelihood of Chinese aggression in the region immediately north or west of Australia.

That strange speech by Gordon Freeth had been authorized by Prime Minister Gorton, whose motives often earned the approval of the Australian people but whose methods just as often lacked finesse. It seems obvious now that Gorton and Freeth wanted to demonstrate that their Government had a mind of its own and was not tied permanently to American defence policy. Nothing ever came of the so-called talks 'involving bilateral relations and wider issues', and the Russians must have been as perplexed as everyone else. Indeed if 'the talks' ever had begun the Russian Embassy in Canberra seemed to have been among the last to have heard of them and 'the talks' do not seem to have continued after Freeth's speech. The conclusion that must be reached is that Freeth's speech was another expression of Gortonian nationalism and that it was intended to resound down the corridors of the Pentagon and to reach the ears of American decision-makers who had shown on other occasions that they would react with alarm every time anyone pushed them on their emotive buttons marked Russia and China.

The clumsiness of the attempt was underlined by the fact that the Australian Minister for Defence, Allen Fairhall, had made a speech only one month earlier which had been a virtual opposite of almost everything that Freeth said. Fairhall had emphasized the dangers posed by the recent entry into the Indian Ocean by the Russian Fleet, and of China's aggressive and threatening stance.

Allen Fairhall correctly viewed that his Government's bluff was ludicrous and could not succeed. It would only bring down upon the head of the Government the anger of bewildered electors. Soon after that Fairhall began to disassociate himself from his own government, and at the end of the year retired to enter private business where people were more predictable.

As Fairhall had expected the U.S. Government disregarded Freeth's speech – although the Soviet Embassy in Canberra spent several smiling weeks attempting to hold the Australian government to its supposed new policy of co-operation. At the general elections at the end of that year the Gorton government narrowly escaped defeat, and Freeth lost his Western Australian seat in Federal Parliament. By way of apology, Prime Minister Gorton found another job for him. He sent Freeth off to Tokyo as Australian ambassador to fill in time around Japanese golf courses until he could make a political comeback – and where no doubt Freeth often pondered ruefully on the consequences of trying to be too tricky in foreign affairs.

The Gorton government, having scraped back into

office, set about repairing the damage to its standing in Western Australia. It promised to upgrade the landing strip at Learmonth in the bush near the U.S. communications base at Exmouth Gulf. This again was only paying lip-service because the government did not intend to station an adequate fighter or bomber force at Learmonth to put knuckles into west coast defence.

The Gorton government also began going through the motions of establishing a naval base at Cockburn Sound near the city of Perth where most of the western voters lived. The first stage, to be built over a leisurely period of years, was to be the construction of a causeway connecting the mainland with an island, thus enclosing a fine body of water as a safe harbour. This would cost all of $9 million. (Three years later it was still being discussed as an unfinished project.) The second stage of the 'naval base' to be undertaken still further in the future would be the construction of facilities to support four escort vessels and three submarines for up to one year, *without dry docking.*

The only naval vessels permanently stationed on the west coast of Australia were a launch and an Attack Class patrol boat. The patrol boat was armed with a small calibre, obsolete anti-aircraft gun, a machine gun and nothing else. All Attack Class patrol boats were bad sea-going vessels and could be outrun by most modern fishing trawlers. Their young crews were ashamed of their uselessness.

As a news correspondent I visited Perth in 1970 with Malcolm Fraser who had replaced the disillusioned Allen Fairhall as Defence Minister. We had been undergoing a press briefing from a senior Navy officer when I asked what would happen if a Navy ship was damaged accidentally or by enemy action in the Indian Ocean. Where would they send it for repairs? There would not be a dry dock available anywhere on the west coast of Australia. The Navy officer went slightly red under his suntan: 'It would have to go to Sydney on the east coast,' he said 'or we could send it to Singapore.'

Later I mentioned to Defence Minister Fraser that the crew of the Attack Class patrol boat at Cockburn Sound had told me that they thought their boat would go faster if it had oars. Fraser reacted like a man trying to hold up a slowly toppling tree. He asked me in exasperation, 'What do you expect us to do? Go out and buy another aircraft carrier?'

Clearly the Australian Government thought that Australian defence of the west coast was impossible and therefore it would not spend any more money on it than was absolutely necessary for appearances and politics. Nothing much had changed in defence outlook in Canberra since 1942 when an Australian general had prepared to abandon all of Australia to the enemy, except for the section of the east coast between Brisbane and Melbourne.

The Australian Government took solace from the fact that the United States had been gathering Australia into its nuclear defence system. By the end of 1971 a number of secret U.S. bases had been established in Australia as 'joint control' establishments. One of these was the communications base at Exmouth which could send signals to nuclear submarines as far west as the Mediterranean. It was on rented ground on the flat and inhospitable west coast, surrounded by low scrub which was infested with poisonous snakes. When cyclones raged along that coast winds of up to 120 miles an hour strained the base to its foundations and drove ocean tidal waves up to one mile inland, sometimes leaving large boats stranded on sandhills. When the seas receded there were salt water lakes around the countryside and scrub and trees festooned with stinking strands of seaweed and in the mud lay many dead fish. A midday summer heat of 110 degrees Farenheit was not unusual at Exmouth and the countryside rapidly dried out. The salt water lakes soon became glistening white salt deposits.

The base consisted of some buildings housing instruments and other equipment, and an administration block and accommodation for single men. Above the buildings were the thirteen communications towers, ranging in height from 996 feet to 1,271 feet – all of them higher than the Eiffel Tower of Paris. It seemed incredible that they could withstand the Australian cyclone season but they had been designed to do just that. People who claimed to know what they were talking about stated that the base on North West Cape at Exmouth was one of a series and was part of the U.S. second-strike capability. They claimed that missiles from nuclear submarines could be triggered off from Exmouth. The U.S. Government never replied to their 'informed' guesses. Exmouth was classified top secret. The only positive piece of additional information I was able to glean while I was there was that if you held a fluorescent tube anywhere within close proximity of the communication towers it would light up in your hand as brightly as if you were part of the power supply. It was not a phenomenon that I was exactly happy to have revealed to me, nor worth a security pass to find out, but evidently it helped to amuse the U.S. sailors on station there to show that they could turn themselves into human electric torches.

Work on the base was begun in 1963 after the Menzies Federal government had taken the land from the Western Australian government. The site was rented to the United States government for one peppercorn – which was solemnly paid by the U.S. Ambassador Ed. Clark, when he attended the official opening of the base in 1967. The base was named after the prime minister who succeeded Menzies and became the Harold E. Holt Base. It was only a courtesy title. No one ever referred to it as that.

By 1972 a total of 1,100 American men, women and children were living at the nearby township of Exmouth and another 400 single U.S. servicemen lived at the base. About 400 Australians from Exmouth worked there every day. Co-existence in the township and on the base between the Australians and Americans was harmonious.

The Australian flag was flying at Exmouth alongside the American flag, this being one of the conditions imposed by the Australian government to lessen public criticism that Australian sovereignty was not being respected. Another condition had been an agreement that the base would be made available to the Australian Navy if ever it needed it, which was good for a hollow laugh most days of the year. There was, however, an Australian Navy officer on duty at Exmouth to maintain an allied presence.

American Navy personnel came and went at Exmouth without the Australian public knowing much about what was happening. Huge Starlifters and other long-range U.S. aircraft could fly in from half way around the world without calling at any major Australian towns where they would attract attention. They arrived regularly from Hawaii or Fiji or from the Philippines, sometimes making a stop-over at Alice Springs in the centre of Australia before touching down at Learmonth, 23 miles south of Exmouth. This so-called Australian air base had a runway so short that the big transports invariably overshot the end of it before stopping in clouds of dust not far from the bush. There was nothing at Learmonth except a few iron huts and red dust and some waiting cars and trucks. U.S. aircrews whimpered and were reluctant to set foot on the ground there. They sought permission to take off again as soon as possible. Between Learmonth and Exmouth the only sights were more scrub, sand, a few kangaroos trying to commit suicide in the middle of the road, and some wild horses which were the descendants of Australian Army cavalry mounts. There was also a fish factory which was tied down with steel cables set into concrete to prevent it from being blown away in the cyclone season.

The Americans could have landed their President and the U.S. Senate at Learmonth for a three day visit and could have had them out again before word of it would have been received in Canberra. Native runners carrying message sticks were faster than the service provided by the single line civilian telephone service from that district.

Few Australians knew anything about a visit to Exmouth in October 1971 by a U.S. Navy board of inquiry which investigated charges against Captain Jess L. Cariker, the commanding officer at the base. After the inquiry Cariker was relieved of his command following his refusal to resign. He was assigned to a Navy hospital in the United States for a medical examination. On his way home Captain Cariker told the Australian Press that he was the victim of a 'Caine mutiny'. He claimed that some junior officers at the base had plotted against him, and that there were theft rings and incompetence at Exmouth and a country club atmosphere which he had tried to end. He added that his efforts to instil more discipline into American personnel had been resisted. The U.S. personnel had 'gone Australian'. Following allegations were made that Captain Cariker had an anti-Australian chip on his shoulder, and that he had insulted the Lord Mayor of Perth during a social occasion at Exmouth. But when Cariker returned to the U.S. one of his own sons remained behind to compete in an Australian spear-fishing contest on the east coast.

The Australian Government made some discreet inquiries into the unhappy affair. Concern was expressed in Australian newspapers that one day a U.S. commander at Exmouth in need of psychiatric treatment could start an action that would land Australia in the middle of the Third World War. Not much heed was paid to the fact that the U.S. government was not overjoyed by such a prospect either. Captain Cariker's replacement was in Exmouth within three days of his transfer orders.

Some of the other U.S. bases in Australia were N.A.S.A. stations that had been designed to do military tracking of satellites. One U.S. Navy tracking station was at Elizabeth in South Australia and another was near an old Cobb and Co. stage coach outpost near Woomera. The most important of all of them was one at Pine Gap, almost in the dead centre of the continent. It also was the most provocative politically. The cloak and dagger security surrounding the place infuriated some people.

Australians did not believe that the governments of the U.S.S.R. or China were being foxed by silence and silliness.

Pine Gap was at the end of a long road out into the desert and was out of bounds to almost all Australians, including most members of the Australian parliament. The Australian flag flew alongside the American flag at Pine Gap but that was meaningless. All the personnel of the base were Americans. It was generally agreed in the Australian press that Pine Gap had been built as part of the U.S. spy satellite system guarding the United States against sudden nuclear attack by long range missiles. It had cost America $200 million.

When Gough Whitlam, the Leader of the Australian Federal Opposition, demanded to be admitted to Pine Gap in 1971, the U.S. Goverment had to be careful. Whitlam was the man who could become prime minister of Australia the following year if his party won the next election. Therefore the Americans could not deny him entry. On the other hand the U.S. government distrusted the Australian Labor Party and believed that some A.L.P. members were a security risk. The Pentagon took seriously all the frequent allegations in Australia that some A.L.P. men were communist-sympathizers, and dossiers were kept on them. The U.S. Embassy in Canberra kept Washington informed of accusations that the A.L.P. was under the influence of communist-controlled trade unions. Thus the U.S. government did not like Whitlam snooping around Pine Gap.

Australians knew that it was absurd to classify Whitlam as a communist-sympathizer. He was in fact more right wing by private inclination than some members of the Liberal Party. But the fact remained that Whitlam led the A.L.P. and was a volatile man with a record for frank and outspoken remarks when angered. The Americans decided that when he visited Pine Gap they would give him as little information as possible.

When the 6 feet 4 inch figure of the Labor leader loomed on the base the Americans, politely and with due deference, showed Whitlam the mess halls and the recreational facilities and the toilet blocks, but did not permit him to see any of the vital equipment or any other important scientific installations. This was an error. On 10 November 1971 the Deputy Leader of the Opposition Lance Barnard complained: 'It is absurd that the Leader of the Opposition Mr Whitlam cannot see these things while it appears that the U.S. Deputy Defence Secretary will be able to walk straight in and see what he likes. It is to be hoped that he sees something of the significant equipment at the base and not just the mess halls, recreation facilities and toilet blocks. These are all that Australian members of parliament, including the leaders of the alternative government, are permitted to see.' Barnard added that when Whitlam visited Pine Gap he should have been trusted.

Whitlam was one of the top political leaders of his country, he was in the middle of his own country, and he was visiting an establishment where his own country's flag was flying. Furthermore he was a lawyer, not a scientist, and did not know a scientific installation from a bull's foot. As long as he had not taken pictures to show the kids at home he would have been harmless.

The overall policy of the Australian government that permitted the Americans to put their space-spy and second-strike communications on Australian territory was open to many questions and doubts as to its wisdom. The government responsible for having granted the initial approval had evidently been convinced that it was being smart by buttoning into the American defence system. At that time Canberra was still recovering from losing Mother Britain and wanted someone else to hold its hand, and at any cost. Now many Australians did not feel any greater amount of security through having the American bases. The United States had not spent hundreds of millions of dollars building them for the benefit of Australia. It had built them for the defence of America. In doing this the Americans had made parts of Australia legitimate military targets for enemies of the United

States, and had done this without having contributed anything specific for Australia's defence. Some intended defence of Australia was implied by the presence of the bases, of course, but there remained a not unreasonable suspicion that Washington's military planners regarded Australia as being just another remote place suitable for forward defence for the United States – their attitude being similar to that of military planners in Canberra who believed that backward countries in South East Asia were useful for the forward defence of Australia.

There was little doubt that from Washington the continent of Australia sometimes looked like a big convenient aircraft carrier, always available for use. The only consolation for insecure Australians was that American investment had painted the Stars and Stripes on it and would not like to see it sunk.

12
Institutional investment

The Australian government had drawn up guidelines relating to local borrowings which encouraged foreign-controlled groups to seek local partnerships in their Australian ventures. The government had also exempted Australian companies from interest-withholding tax. Foreign-controlled companies in Australia were required to pay the tax. The results, however, had not been satisfactory from Australia's viewpoint.

As early as 1965 two Australian economists, Fitzpatrick and Wheelwright, had given their opinion that there had been too rich an infusion of American dollars into Australia for the nation to digest. They had claimed that it was bad for the continued health and growth of the economy, and for the social and political community of Australia. They were afraid that Australia would lose its 'distinctive character'.

Two years later an outspoken Labor member of the Australian Parliament, Tom Uren, made his diagnosis. 'A growing cancer of overseas capital,' he declared during a speech in the House, 'is eating into Australia's national heritage.' Uren unsuccessfully argued for the formation of an all-Party committee to inquire into all aspects of overseas investment in the country.

'My God,' said Ed Clarke (the American Ambassador in Canberra), in a private conversation with me one day, 'they forget that English investment money helped to make Texas what it is today. If I buy into an Australian industry it doesn't mean that I'll be able to pick it up and carry it back to the U.S. It'll have to stay right here.' The superficial logic of this made him bellow with laughter. In private life Clarke was a Texas banker.

Some naive Australians had wanted to believe that American businessmen were in their country because they wished to help Australia. But with slow reluctance they accepted the truth that most of the Americans were in Australia to help themselves – and that some of them were doing it with both hands.

In July 1967, Edgar F. Kaiser arrived in Australia in person, all steamed up and ready to defend himself and other American investors. Kaiser said that if overseas capital was blocked, as some Australians advocated, development in Australia would stagnate again. Flashing gold cuff links and bracelets, and glaring through his spectacles, the tycoon snapped that he was in Australia to inspect his company's $200 million investments which he expected to increase. He added sternly that Australians had to realize that although U.S. companies took profits out of the country they also paid big taxes and royalties to the Australian government. 'You are better off by using overseas investment,' Kaiser said. 'You can't just sit here and do nothing.' Kaiser predicted that the tremendous industrial development along the west coast of the United States would require supplies of iron ore and coal from Australia to keep it going. Australians squirmed when he said that. They were playing the role of suppliers to the heavy industries of Japan already and they were sick and tired of it. Kaiser evidently thought that he would be doing them a favour by extending this role to the U.S., but they believed that the road he was indicating was not the way to Australian greatness. It was no longer any use Kaiser telling Australians that they were all great friends and got along just fine. Friendship existed in business only when everyone remained successful and convinced that their future was secure.

The pro-American Liberals in Canberra kept out of the national debate on foreign investment as much as was possible, but some members of the Australian government shared the uneasiness of the Labor opposition. The Minister for National Development in 1967, David Fairbairn, warned American and British companies engaged in the offshore search for oil along the Australian coast that they would be well advised to seek an Australian participation in their ventures. More of the offshore areas were owned by foreign companies than his government wanted. Fairbairn added that nothing turned a country against overseas investment as much as companies within the country which were 100 per cent foreign-owned.

The retiring chief of Fairbairn's own department, Sir Harold Raggatt, claimed, however, that Australian companies were too timid to invest in big operations in the early risk stages, Raggatt had been visited by representatives of almost every foreign oil and mining company contemplating investment in Australia. Almost all had sought Australians as partners, and some of them had been ready to become the minor partners. But when Raggatt had suggested the names of Australian companies who might be interested he had usually found that the foreign companies had already made an unsuccessful approach to them.

Foreign ownership bothered the rough and sometimes ready John Grey Gorton, a man of the Australian people. Gorton was a nationalist who wanted to ensure that Australians could continue to control their country and its assets. As Prime Minister of Australia from 1969 to 1971 he had a lot to worry about because those were the years when Australia was being bought and sold. Gorton sometimes made autocratic decisions. Unfortunately he did not have much patience nor the desire to linger over details nor was he fluent in explaining what he had done or why he had done it. When he felt the need to take strong action against foreign investment he attacked the problem and drew blood – but he slashed only at the most obvious and convenient targets. The wounds he inflicted were superficial and not of lasting advantage to his nation.

In 1968 the Sun Alliance Group had seemed about to acquire the Australian insurance company, M.L.C. – an economic complex which had one of the most important network of investments in Australia. Prime

Minister Gorton believed that such a takeover would not be in the best interests of his country. Accordingly he moved fast and passed a law to protect Australian ownership of the M.L.C. and its assets. He explained that the non-life insurance industry of Australia was already dominated by overseas groups, leaving only the life sector of the industry under local control. 'Too authoritative!' Gorton's political enemies shouted. 'You protected M.L.C., but you did it like an American president.'

Later, Gorton believed that he had to protect the Australian uranium industry. Queensland Mines, an exploratory company, had discovered what was reputed to be one of the world's richest deposits of uranium in the Northern Territory. The Prime Minister took legislative action to restrict foreign investment in the company. Immediately his critics again threw up their hands in horror, claiming that this time Gorton had intruded into the sanctity of company ownership and investment like a Labor man.

Gorton's demonstrated readiness to get tough with big business became an important part of the Liberal's decision to rid themselves of his leadership. Nationalism riding roughshod over business and investment was not a safe gallop for a Liberal prime minister at any time. But there were many Australians who took off their hats to Gorton's cavalier nationalism, no matter how inexpertly he exercised it.

To reveal that Prime Minister Gorton had skimmed over the depths of American financial strength in Australia, a Labor leader, Frank Crean, declared in Parliament that he had evidence that U.S. investment in Australia was doubling cumulatively every five years. Crean warned that the Australian government had not been keeping itself sufficiently well informed about the rate of expansion of American investment.

Crean's quiet remarks carried weight. He was the man who would become Australia's Federal Treasurer – if he were still in Parliament when Labor next formed a government.

Back in 1942 a Labor government had passed a law prohibiting foreign banks from opening branches in Australia. It had been about as successful as putting up a barbed wire fence to stop the overflow from a dam. In a penetrating series of articles published in 1971 in the *Australian Financial Review*, Mr M. W. Acheson IV, the assistant vice president of the Bankers Trust Company of New York, explained how American and other foreign banks had established what he described as 'a meaningful presence' in Australia. They had done it legally by infiltrating into the non-trading bank sectors of the Australian financial infrastructure. A total of ninety-five foreign banking institutions had opened for business in Australia through local representatives or through investments in merchant banks, finance companies, or other financial organizations. By 1971 these foreign banks represented total assets equivalent to well over $A500,000 million. Mr Acheson pointed out whimsically that this was five times the cumulative total gross national expenditure in Australia over the four years up to 1971, about eighty times the total assets of the Australian banking system, and several hundred times greater than the total reserve position of the Australian Treasury.

Foreign banks justified their investments in Australia as being necessary to service other foreign businesses which also had investments in Australia. But Australia offered investors a unique climate of stable and predictable economic, political, and social conditions – while at the same time offering tremendous potential growth, particularly in the mining industry. Mr Acheson added, 'It is plain to see that in the face of such mineral wealth ... supported and complemented by booming industrial conditions ... overseas investors have been stumbling over one another in a somewhat undignified rush to share in Australia's manifest destiny'.

Of the foreign banks in Australia by 1971 fourteen U.S. banks, eight Japanese banks, four French, three Swiss, and two U.K. banks had representatives in Australia. In the process of foreign banks seeking to establish themselves in Australia, U.S. banks had become share-holders in seventeen Australian merchant banks, British banks in sixteen and Japanese in six.

Some of the foreign banks looked around for reputable Australian partners to form entirely new merchant banks in Australia. Typical of these had been the partnership of the Sydney stock brokers, Ord Minnett, T. J. Thompson and Partners with Bankers Trust Company of New York to form Ord-B.T. Company Limited. Melbourne stock brokers, A. C. Goode, joined Chase Manhattan Bank in forming Chase-N.B.A.

The long-established trading banks of Australia had seen their opportunity and had joined foreign banks to form additional merchant banks. Thus the Bank of New South Wales had joined the Bank of America and the Bank of Tokyo to form Partnership Pacific Limited, and the National Bank had combined with the Chase Manhattan Bank and the A. C. Goode Alliance to form Chase-N.B.A. Limited. Wells Fargo Bank of San Francisco had headed out into the west to form its own Australian merchant bank with no local shareholders.

Foreign investment in merchant banking and the finance establishments of Australia constituted the massive base of the iceberg about which the Australian public knew almost nothing. It had been expanding tremendously, almost unnoticed by the Australian government and while members of parliament had been pre-occupied with and squawking about the company investment scene showing above the surface. While fears were still being expressed in parliament about the possibility that foreign money would own Australia at some time in the future that possibility already had happened.

American banks just loved Australia. Back home in the United States there were stringent limitations on their expansion. Some of the U.S. banks could not move out of one building, or out of one city or out of one State. For example, a bank in California could not open up branches in New York City, nor could it expand its services and range by acquiring other American financial institutions without meeting resistance, difficult regulatory problems, or outright refusal by the authorities. For them Australia was the wide new frontier, innocent and unfenced, where they could career headlong in any direction they pleased.

Another factor causing their rush to Australia was that the potential return on investment in Australia was greater than at home. In 1970 the top ten U.S. banks showed an average return on shareholders' funds after tax of 11.3 per cent. The average return after tax on shareholders' funds for the major finance companies in Australia was 13.4 per cent.

The First National City Bank of New York was cited as having won the prize for the most ambitious and aggressive invasion of Australia's financial markets. It had set up a network comprised of an overseas investment corporation, two large finance companies and a merchant bank, a holding company, and an unofficial and an official money market dealer. It had invested up to $A45 million in Australia, not including its Australian loan portfolio and its contingent liability to provide another $A45 million in stand-by credit facilities. It stood astride local capital markets like an Alsatian holding down a Pekingese.

By mid 1971 none of the best money-making opportunities in Australia had escaped the U.S. banks or other international financiers. Their tentacles had probed into everything. Overseas banks were specializing in leasing and were also moving into venture capital. In leasing, the Morgan Guaranty Trust of New York owned a third of Financial Leasing Corporation, along with Australian United Corporation in which it had 15 per cent and the Bank of Adelaide's finance company, Finance Corporation of Australia. The First National Bank of Boston owned 50 per cent of First Leasing Australia Limited. Wallace Brothers of London had joined C.A.G.A. (which was 20 per cent owned by the Bank of America) and Patrick and Company in acquiring Dier Computer Corporation from Bankers Trust Company . . . and so on into the tangled brambles of Australia's fast-growing financial jungle.

All possibilities of future profit were being covered as well as current returns. For example, in the venture capital field a group of American businessmen had joined Australians in a company called Technology Resource Development Limited with the intention of providing financial, technical, and management support for young Australian enterprises seeking to take advantage of technological developments. And a foreign group including Evlyn de Rothschild had formed International Venture Corporation Pty Limited to invest in small Australian companies demonstrating attractive growth potential.

Economists had been complaining throughout 1971 that the over-valued U.S. dollar had been finding too easy a haven in Australia. Of course, the development of big industries in any country demanded big financial backing. Only international financing could give Australia that kind of support. In addition, foreign banks had brought a level of financial expertise and strength into Australia which it had lacked previously. One result of this had been the growing use by Australian companies of foreign loan capital, especially Euro-dollars, which had been introduced mainly by foreign bankers. American business and financial managers had also begun training their Australian colleagues and subordinates to higher efficiency. The standard of top management in Australia had not been in international class, except for some notable exceptions, and an influx of expert tutors was worth having. But despite all of this Australian economists remained unhappy about what was happening.

Foreign bankers frequently expressed their hopes that there would be a continuance of peaceful co-existence with local financial interests. It was difficult to see their hopes not being realized as they owned a piece of almost every local financial house. Yet the foreign bankers had been cautious. They had made sure that the pieces they owned were not yet too big. More than 60 per cent of the merchant banks in Australia in which they had invested had a local equity of 50 per cent or more.

The Americans and other foreign bankers would have
been unwisely optimistic, however, had they believed that
the frontier days of Australian finance would continue
indefinitely. Some Australian government was going to
have to control their activities at some time within the
fairly near future as had been done long ago in the
United States and elsewhere. There was danger to any
country in too much and too easy a reliance on an un-
controlled and unplanned capital inflow. It led to foreign
investors having too much command over the policies
and destinies of industries.

The Australian Treasurer, Billy Snedden, claimed glibly
in 1971 that the high rate of capital inflow was an encouraging indication of continuing confidence in the
future of Australia – and some chauvinists believed him.
It would have been truer if Snedden had said that much
of it reflected an inflow of international bargain-hunters
into the Australian equity market, an inflow of foreign
money manipulators, and the temporary lodging of
American money to escape taxation in the United States.
This had been making domestic economic management by
the government a bad joke. The long-lasting Liberal-
Country Party government always seemed to want to
dodge past anything that was complex or required deep
and thoughtful planning, and preferred to look for easier
solutions which often turned out to be totally inadequate
in the long term. Snedden's comment was extremely
amateurish.

Australia's financial newspapers kept telling the government that international money that flowed easily into
a country was likely to flow out again just as easily and
as quickly if, for example, there was an unfavourable
revaluation in the Australian currency. The more international banking became the more the movements of
money in and out of a country became merely a series
of book entries. This was a major problem that the
government had to face in exchange controls but which
it was ignoring by looking the other way. The Australian
securities industry had to go international both internally

and externally. Someone had to do something – and 1972 became the year for it.

The Australian Senate had once been a dull place – little more than a comfortable club where elderly men dozed and burped after dinnner or made rambling speeches to which no one listened. It had been operating sluggishly for many years as a house of review to double check legislation passed by the House of Representatives. But one day the honourable senators had awakened to the realization that if they used the committee inquiry system of the U.S. Senate as a model they could do much more to increase their usefulness and importance. They began setting up committees to investigate numerous aspects of Australian life. They had committees on drug trafficking, inquiries into scandals on the stock exchange, or into the shooting of kangaroos, or into the search for oil off the Australian coast. Under public acclaim the senators warmed to their work and thought less of the extra $25 a day they could earn on committees service. Frequently they made headlines with their close questioning and in the process upset some of the sacred cows of the Australian Establishment. Prominent men who had believed themselves not to be answerable to anyone for their actions, and who the law had not been able to touch, suddenly found themselves sweating under cross-examination before a senate committee and with journalists taking down every word they said.

With the support of the D.L.P., a minority party, the Australian Labor Party won a majority in the Senate to establish a select committee to inquire into foreign investment in Australia and to make recommendations on whether the rate of foreign investment should be controlled. The alarmed fluttering of investment and other financial institutions all over the country and abroad could be sensed in the Senate Chamber as the belated decision was made despite the protestations of the government leader, Sir Kenneth Anderson, who appealed to the senators to ask themselves whether they were not already doing too much work.

If the House of Representatives could no longer operate as efficiently as a House of government should, due to its miserably obstructive party system, the senators had to take up more of the burden. It was little wonder that they had so much work to do. A great number of questions needed to be asked about the way that the country was being run.

The attitude of the Liberal-Country Party government had been that if American and other foreign investment was examined too closely it would cringe like a novice nun caught in the nude and would flee, never to be seen in Australia again. The Australian Labor Party, on the other hand, suspected that a searching inquiry would reveal no such shy maiden but would disclose a hairy-arsed ogre who would have to be hit with an axe before it would take its paw out of the cookie jar.

Prime Minister McMahon announced that the Treasury Department was preparing its own inquiry into foreign investment and would issue a White Paper – a genteel manoeuvre seen as a possible counter to the Senate Select Committee. The Senate was at odds on to uncover more and to make it more public. Meanwhile, down at the Treasury disgruntled senior officers were quietly working on another submission for the better management of the government's own money. They intended to ask that some budgetry items and expenditure on them be planned over three years instead of annually. They hoped to remove at least some of the national revenue beyond reach of politicians who treated every annual Federal Budget as being primarily an object with which to catch votes like some kind of butterfly net.

However, it became evident that foreign investment was to be an important issue in the 1972 Australian elections and what started out as a reluctant move by the McMahon government soon gathered momentum. The Government's Bureau of Census and Statistics was set to work digging up as much information about foreign investment in as short a time as possible. Senior officers in the Bureau grumbled that they had been set a gigantic task at short notice, but all conceded that it was better for the Government to know a little about the ownership of their country than nothing at all.

The project became top priority and by March the Government was able to make public the first results of its research – a directory of 205 pages and listing almost 1,000 Australian industrial firms which had substantial foreign ownership. It was the first such directory in Australia since 1966, but because of the great haste in which it had been compiled much of the information in it was hopelessly outdated. For example, the breakdown of the extent of overseas ownership and control was one to two years earlier than the time of publication. Details in it of overall foreign interests were mouldy. They were for the years 1966-7, and thus were virtually useless except as an historic record. However, so ignorant was the Australian public that even some of these old facts came as a shock.

American businessmen operating in Australia rightly began to fear that the Australian Government was at last considering stringent controls on overseas holdings in Australian companies as part of Australia's growing 'economic nationalism'. They saw it as significant that the public release of the Government's company directory had co-incided with the opening of the first South Pacific meeting of the Asian Pacific Council of American Chambers of Commerce. It was being held in Canberra and was being attended by U.S. delegates from ten Asian and Pacific countries.

The Americans at the conference probably knew more collectively about foreign investment in Australia than did the Australian government. Certainly the United States Embassy did not need to refer to a directory based on out-of-date figures. The American Ambassador, W. L. Rice, was able to tell the conference with an air of quiet pride and certainty that he had information which revealed that *at least a third of all manufactured goods exported by Australia were produced by firms with substantial U.S. ownership.*

The American delegates at the conference approached their self-appointed task of lobbying in Canberra in their typical well-practised and practical manner. They set out to prepare submissions to the Senate Select Committee on Foreign Ownership and Control – which they clearly recognized as the greater of the two-pronged danger facing their profits. The Secretary of the conference, William Rosenthal said sadly, 'For too long we've seldom told everyone of all the good we do. A balance sheet approach now might be a darned good way to show the assets and liabilities – including pollution and so on. On balance we think we should be able to show a net gain. We have a strong case to support our contention that international investment contributes positively to countries.'

Rosenthal was echoing what other Americans were then saying elsewhere in the world in defence against growing criticism of the operations of international corporations. In Canada, an example of this criticism had been a recent statement by the Canadian Secretary of State for External Affairs, Mitchell Sharp, that some multi-national corporations were imperialistic and treated their foreign operations as colonial outposts of the home office.

In Canberra, Ambassador Rice warned that Australian controls of foreign investment could hobble Australia's 'mineral development'. He then complained that one American firm had spent $A60 million looking for oil in Australia and Papua New Guinea without finding any. But Rice was going to need to come up with something better than a hard luck story like that to soften the growing spirit of head-hunting now rising in the Australian Parliament.

During the same week, Herbert P. Patterson, President of the U.S. Chase Manhattan Bank had just announced that Chase Manhattan had taken a 32.75 per cent interest in the Sydney finance company, Alliance Holdings Limited. Patterson said he believed that economic rather than political issues would most dramatically affect relations between the United States and its friends in the Pacific area over the following year. Evidently he was concerned about what that effect would be because he added, 'No country I know has been taken over politically because of economic investment.'

One of the most outstanding of the younger politicians in Canberra was the leader of the Country Party, Douglas Anthony. He told the conference of American chambers of commerce, that the Australian government was aware of the possibility that companies which were controlled overseas could adopt the practice of exporting goods from Australia at cost, including raw materials, and that these could then be used as 'inputs' for their industries in foreign countries – and that this was not necessarily in Australia's best interests. The blond-haired, athletic Anthony was putting forward the proposition in his mild way that a U.S. company which owned a smelter in South Korea or Taiwan could ensure that it received Australian ore at the cheapest prices by buying the company mining the Australian ore – although Anthony was too polite to spell it out like that.

The American audience listening to Anthony got the message. The Rip Van Winkle Government of Canberra had finally woken up.

13
The illusion of progress

At the end of the 1960s a wild boom on Australian stock markets brought in millions of dollars of gambling money from foreign speculators and from the Australian public. Brokers and company principals with inside information and stock market expertise made fortunes. There had only to be a brief mention of the rumour of a nickel strike in Western Australia to double within one day the share prices of all companies with leases in the same area. School boys skipped their classes to go down to the stock exchanges to invest their accumulated pocket money. Housewives and labourers brushed shoulders with shopgirls and businessmen in the public viewing galleries at the stock exchanges, sometimes fighting for better positions from which to watch through binoculars the price fluctuations on the boards. They struggled for possession of telephones to tell their brokers to buy or sell.

The smarter ones and the luckier got out early with their winnings. The majority stayed in the game and went down with the share bust of 1970 and 1971, amid a welter of reports of company failures and swindles and crooked dealing. Some who had bought in at the peak of the market with their life savings were left holding shares worth only one tenth of the prices they had paid for them. Some shares sank to half a cent each. Others vanished from the exchange boards into oblivion.

The craziness on the stock exchanges was typified by the experience of shareholders in Poseidon Limited. In 1969 Poseidon struck it rich in nickel in Western Australia. The price of its shares had been only 60 cents, but it took off like a rocket roaring to the moon and hit $214 a share later that year, and $280 the following year.

But by late 1971 Poseidon had dwindled in price back down to $11. It had been a great ride up for those who had seen their shares multiplied in value 460 times, but not so good on the way down for those who had paid $280 and who saw their share reduced in value to one-twenty-fifth of their cost.

Other public investors lost heavily when a hole in the desert owned by Tasminex was also alleged to have struck rich nickel. 'It could be bigger and better than Poseidon,' a company director declared to newsmen. Possibly he was talking only about the hole, but the Tasminex shares which had been at 50 cents in 1969 had soared to $90 by 1970. Helicopters loaded with suspicious journalists and representatives of mining rivals frequently hovered over the isolated and closely guarded drilling area of Tasminex, but were prevented from making a closer investigation. Nothing much ever did come out of that hole, but as the Tasminex shares slowly sank optimists among the public continued to buy them all the way down. Before the end of the year the shares were looking greatly overpriced at $1.50.

And once upon a time there was another Australian company called Leopold which reported having a core sample revealing high promise of yet another western nickel strike. Up shot the Leopold shares. Oddly enough no one ever was able to find that core sample, although the police helped in a search for it. There was a lot of trouble over that incident, and another issue of heart-break for investors.

One of the saddest casualties of the mining boom was Mineral Securities, an Australian investment complex which had been the hope of Australian nationalists. The chief of Mineral Securities, Ken McMahon, had become a popular hero of the stock exchanges because of the brilliance of his footwork as he climbed. He had acquired large holdings for Mineral Securities in a choice selection of key mining assets in Australia. One of his avowed aims was to prevent these assets from getting into foreign hands. Alas, Ken McMahon stumbled and fell into a deep crevasse taking with him Mineral Securities and its many wide-eyed trusting shareholders who were financially roped to him. He fell because his amb'tion had over-reached his resources. He had made the elementary mistake of borrowing short and investing long. Mineral Securities smashed into pieces on the rocks.

The fragments retrieved by the liquidator who acted as mortician were still large and extremely valuable. They included holdings in the great Robe River iron ore deposits in Western Australia and in the uranium deposits of Kathleen Investments and Queensland Mines. The liquidator had to call for tenders to buy these holdings to pay off the liabilities of Mineral Securities. Those able to submit the highest tenders were the big foreign companies who pounced like vultures onto a carcase. American interests picked up Robe River shares while Noranda of Canada swooped onto Kathleen Investments and shared with the A.M.P. Society the pickings on Queensland Mines.

Queensland Mines was the company which Prime Minister Gorton had tried to protect from a foreign take-over through legislation. It had announced a uranium reserve of 55,000 tons of uranium oxide, with an assay averaging 450 lb a ton – the richest uranium deposit in the world. Investors had stampeded to pay a peak of $43 a share for Queensland Mines. Noranda of Canada paid only around $23 a share for the holdings relinquished by the shattered Mineral Securities and thought it had made a good deal. Australians groaned.

However, on Friday the thirteenth in August 1971 – and while Australian nationalists were still bemoaning the news that Noranda of Canada had obtained a slice of Queensland Mines at half price – a terrible thing happened to foreign investment. The board of Queensland Mines gently revealed that a mistake had been made somehow in the original estimate of the reserves of uranium ore at Nabarlek. Instead of the assay averaging out at 540 lb a ton for the bulk of the ore as had been publicly stated, the average now had been brought back down to only 16 lb a ton. This had reduced the known reserves of uranium oxide at Nabarlek from 55,000 tons to only 8,960 tons. The board's announcement was not accompanied by any explanation of how the error had been made – although a great deal of explaining would be required later.

Noranda of Canada had not exactly bought a lemon when it had picked up the Mineral Securities' investment in Queensland Mines, but now it certainly did not look a bargain at $23 a share. One could imagine Ken McMahon's expression when he heard about it, and the feelings of Terry Rogers of Noranda as he quit the board of Queensland Mines.

The stock slump so disgusted Australian investors that they put what remained of their money into the banks or returned to punting on the racetracks. The stock exchanges and their activities stank in Australia's nostrils worse than the fish markets on the eve of Good Friday.

The withdrawal of public support had an unfortunate effect on Australia's leading industrial shares. Even the best of blue chip stocks were wallowing like sick whales. In early 1972 about 63 per cent of the shares listed in Australia were selling for less than ten times their annual earnings. American and other foreign investors again closed in quickly to pick up the best of such shares. The Dow Jones average in New York sold at 16.4 times earnings while in London the equivalent index was 16.9 times earnings.

A former Australian treasurer, Les Bury, warned Australians that 60 per cent of industrial shares on stock exchanges in Australia in December 1971 had been selling at a market price which was less than asset value. Bargain basement prices were being offered for the best of Australia's industrial structure, and it seemed the country was becoming vulnerable to foreign take-overs.

The concept of local Australian participation in the investment field had wilted.

The scene at the stock exchanges – exultation or

despondency – was only the froth on top of an investment situation which was bubbling with steadily rising temperature. Nor did the agitation of the Labor Party or the sporadic warnings of the Australian government make much difference. Foreign money was pouring in. The preponderance of money for portfolio investment was British, but the major portion for financing and development was American.

It was the business of government to make sure that private enterprise of any kind did not operate against the best national interest. But governments which placed their own interests before the best national interests were ineffectual watchdogs. Worse than that, they sometimes helped to sell out important national assests for little more than peanuts. It had often happened in Australia that the State governments were more concerned with their own interests than with the overall national good, leaving it to the Commonwealth government to superintend or correct what they did – if it could, and if it knew about it in time, and then only against fiercest State opposition. Some of the States still behaved as they had when they were separate colonies before Federation and when they had erected tariff barriers against each other.

A notorious example of State government selfishness was the Clutha Development Act, passed by the N.S.W. Government in 1970. This legislation was designed specifically to permit a wholly-owned American company, Clutha Development Pty Limited, to carry off at least eight million tons of coking coal each year from reserves near Sydney and sell the coal to Japan. The Clutha Development Act gave the company the right to build a private railway forty miles long from coal deposits in Burragorang Valley to the Illawarra coast, and to establish a coal dump of anything up to one million tons of coal on top of a 1,300 feet high cliff overlooking the ocean, nearby tourist areas and surfing beaches. From the dump the coal was to be taken by conveyor and along a trestleway extending a mile out into the ocean where it would be emptied into Japanese bulk carriers.

The public outcry over this was based mainly on aesthetic and environmental objections. People complained that the coal dump on the cliff and the ocean trestleway would spoil the superb view along the Illawarra coast which was one of the last areas of coastline in its natural state close to Sydney. The company's plans were akin to building proposals for an iron foundry in the middle of a high class residential suburb.

A public relations officer for Clutha, trying to make the best of his brief, stated that although the project would mean some change in the natural scenery of the Illawarra coast the industrial alterations would be well worthwhile coming to see. He added persuasively: 'What could be a more splendid sight than a bulk carrier of 100,000 tons anchored off your coast?'

It was evident to everyone but Clutha and the N.S.W. government that the very worst aspects of both American industrialization and foreign investment were represented here. Pathetic little groups of protesters stood on top of the cliff at the site of the proposed coal dump. They threw coal dust and released balloons into the high winds which were prevalent in that area to demonstrate that fine coal dust from the proposed dump must be blown down into the suburbs of the neighbourhood city of Wollongong and would soil its surfing beaches, or would be blown north to foul the bushlands of a national park, and probably some of it would drift over the national park and would descend onto the southern suburbs of Sydney.

It was the type of wart on the environment which people in the United States were regretting and which was costing millions of dollars to remedy.

The strategic and industrial stupidity of permitting such foreign activities did not have quite the same impact upon the Australian public. It would be brought home to them at some future time when the long-departed politicians of the N.S.W. government would be beyond a deserved stoning. It was true that Australia had some of the largest reserves in the world of coking coal; but the world's reserves were diminishing like snow in the summer – to the point where there soon would be an overall shortage of coal. This was precisely why Japanese bulk carriers would visit the Australian coast to take away Australian coal mined for them by an American company. At the rate of mining proposed by Clutha, the convenient and easily won deposits of high class coal – right on the doorstep of Australia's centre of heavy industries and population – would be exhausted within twenty years. Presumably the scenery of the Illawarra coast then would be restored to its natural condition. The Japanese bulk ships would call no more to excite the watchers from the cliffs – but the Australian heavy industries of the area would be hunting far abroad for coal to replace that taken from the holes in the ground only fifty miles away.

Of course, it could be argued that within twenty years' time coal would not be in demand for steelworks or anything else, and that it would have been replaced by a more modern fuel. One would have to agree. The very scarcity of the stuff within twenty years would have forced a search for alternatives. But coal was a much more versatile material beyond burning in furnaces. Within twenty years its chemical values would set scientists weeping at the thought of the billions of tons of it which had been shovelled into furnaces. Australia should have been setting aside reserves for that time. Meanwhile, if any coal was to be exported, it should be from the numerous other deposits in Australia more difficult to reach, not from shallow depths right next to an industrial city.

The financial side of the Clutha deal was also worthy of critical examination by Australians. In its hurry to get pocket money to build gutters and drains and a new government office or two in choking Sydney, the N.S.W. government had agreed to accept from Clutha Development a franchise payment likely to be $5 million a year over the following twenty years. The intriguing information made public was that the franchise payment had been based on a fixed amount per ton. This meant that the government's share would remain the same even if the Australian currency depreciated during the next twenty years to half of present values, or if the price of coking coal doubled – the latter possibility being extremely likely.

The American multi-millionaire, Mr Daniel K. Ludwig, who owned Clutha Development Pty Limited, could confidently expect to make profits running into hundreds of millions of dollars. His returns from the sale of the Australian coal were not fixed. He knew that with every increase of $1 a ton in the value of coal as it became scarcer he would make an additional $8 million a year.

The legal liberties which the N.S.W. Government had taken in drafting the Clutha Development Act were scathingly condemned by an eminent lawyer, Mr Edward St John Q.C. who described it as being probably the most controversial piece of legislation ever to become law in Australia. St John drew public attention to the extraordinary privileges bestowed by the Act. Mr Ludwig had been authorized to take with the help of the government, such lands as he required for his private railway and the associated works. He had what amounted to an open invitation to mine what coal he pleased from the Burragorang reserves. He could ship the coal through his own private port, controlled by himself and not by the Government's Maritime Services Board. St John was of the opinion that a whole system of rights and safeguards belonging to the public and to various public bodies had been swept aside to make way for Clutha. These included provision of the town and country planning legislation which gave local authorities and the State Planning Authority power to control development in the area, and provisions of the Mining Act which gave the public the right of objection and appeal, and provisions relating to the acquisition of land for railways.

Scientists had predicted that the development of Clutha's project would cause serious pollution of air and waters, including the Sydney drinking water supply – and the ocean, and destruction of marine life. Massive pollution would also be caused in the Burragorang Valley, formerly another scenic holiday resort. No provision had been made under the Act for protection of the coastal roadstead area or of beaches or of the valley.

St John mentioned, as an important issue, the question of whether a foreign-owned firm should be given such a large slice of the public domain to the evident detriment of the public. Others asked why the N.S.W. government had been so lenient and generous. Everyone knew that Clutha Development Pty Limited would not lend itself to graft, and that the N.S.W. parliamentarians were entirely above any possibility of corruption as were the angels. But that bad odour in the air was not coal gas.

The Chairman of the Joint Coal Board, Mr B. W. Hartnell, took the unusual step in July 1971 of defending Mr Daniel Ludwig in a public statement which came close to being an eulogy. He said that the coal mining industry of eastern Australia owed a great deal to Mr Ludwig. Mr Hartnell then tried to explain exactly what Australians owed to Mr Ludwig. He said that Mr Ludwig had invested large sums of money in the coal mining industry through Clutha Development Pty Limited and as a result of this he had made a major contribution to 'our national prosperity'. Clutha, said Mr Hartnell, had held out strongly and successfully for higher prices to be paid for 'our' coal by the Japanese steel industry. Clutha's management of its open-cut mining in the Upper Hunter district north of Sydney, when there had been overproduction generally, had been wise, helpful and widely applauded. Mr Hartnell reminded Australians that Clutha exported more coal than any other producer – as well as selling some coal to local users. It had operations in five different localities of Australia, and was mining at depth in Queensland. (One would ask here why it was necessary to let Clutha take Sydney coal when it already had such a large piece of the action elsewhere.) In conclusion Hartnell delivered some gratuitous praise 'Mr Ludwig's willingness to spend his money here is undoubtedly one of the coal industry's greatest assets.'

Evidently Hartnell believed that an American who was willing to spend his money in Australia for his own benefit was some new kind of philanthropist. Hartnell's reference to Ludwig's mining operations as making a major contribution to 'our national prosperity' was part of the strange and specious notion which had been implanted into the minds of Australian governments and their officials that all new industry was good for its own sake, quite apart from the aspect of profit or what damage it did, or what unhappiness it caused. Viewed in this light they never questioned any new industry in their country as possibly being undesirable exploitation, or unsatisfactory for the Australian people.

Mostly the Australian people permitted themselves to be persuaded to go along with that view. They had seen their country lying dormant for a lifetime. They had been brought up on vague assertions that something should be done about it, and now wryly took pride in seeing new mines, coal heaps, machinery depots and smoke stacks appearing around the countryside. These signs of industry seemed to be exciting indications that their country was getting ahead.

They were being conned again.

It was regrettable that this tragic and wicked philosophy had taken root in Australia: the philosophy of the industrial revolution of Europe, of the industrial expansion in the United States of an earlier era, and of the new industrialization in Asia. That philosophy was that people were there to serve industry. It had left terrible unhappiness and violence wherever it had been practised in the world, and now it was in Australia. Older industrial nations had awakened to its inhumanity and had been trying to introduce reforms to eliminate it or to ease its cruelties. It was the unarguable duty of industry to serve the people, and not the other way around.

No one had yet stated this strongly enough in Australia where life until recently had been leisurely and pleasant and uncomplicated, compared with conditions in less fortunate countries. Australian trade unions, seeking to preserve their workers' paradise but seeing it moving further out of reach, remained unsure of what could be lost. The unions placed greatest emphasis on the traditional issues with which they were most familiar but seemed largely oblivious to more insidious dangers to the future comfort and happiness of themselves and their families. Coal miners in the Burragorang Valley were strongly in favour of the Clutha Act. To them it simply meant more jobs.

However, the unusually stubborn opposition to the Clutha scheme by other sectors of the public and the publicity given to the important issues involved resulted in plans for an inquiry at Federal level in Canberra in 1972. At such an inquiry it would have been certain that many aspects of American investment in Australia would have been raised in passing and there was no telling where it could have led. But on 9 February 1972, and before a Federal probe could begin, the Clutha struggle came to a sudden end. The company announced that it had abandoned the whole project and asked the N.S.W. government to break the agreement authorized by the Clutha Development Act. The company stressed that it had not caved in under public pressures, but had made its decision because a feasibility study had shown that it would not be economic to proceed with the project. One would have thought, of course, that the company would have made such a feasibility study before deciding to start. Another reason given in Clutha's explanation was a cut-back in Japanese orders for coal – and that sounded more convincing. The N.S.W. government had to accept the company's decision – but still refused to admit that there had been anything wrong with the scheme in the first place.

Strange decisions made by the State government of hillbilly Queensland in mid-1972 permitted another big American company to undercut its competitors including Clutha in the Australian bonanza. The Utah Development Company was expected to earn up to $A940 million from exports of Queensland coking coal in association with its minority partner, Mitsubishi Developments Pty. Ltd. The Queensland government had granted to Utah low rail freight rates and had fixed the royalty payment on the coal at 5 cents a ton!

The Queensland government's claim that the 5 cents royalty would be offset by rail freight profits was absurd. The deal was splendid for Utah – but the people of Australia should have demanded a Royal Commission to investigate why the Queensland government was so poor at arithmetic. Of course suspicion of graft was again unbelievable.

After the botch that had been made of government in Australia since the Second World War the tasks facing any new and responsible government were daunting. Some of the most important problems concerning Australia's future welfare had arisen out of 'frontier' investment in mining, Australia's greatest industry. By 1971 almost 70 per cent of all mining operations in Australia had become foreign-controlled, and a great amount of this by Americans. In that kind of investment American businessmen could not be expected to care too much about the best interests of Australia. They simply sold the commodities they owned in Australia to the highest bidder anywhere at all and for as long as they were permitted to do it. But they had become so established in Australia that it was going to be hard doing anything to stop them.

The Australian public was informed impressively that Australia's mineral production had reached a record value of more than $1,500 million in 1971, and was rising at 25 per cent annually. But the Australian public was *not* being reminded at the same time that almost 70 per cent of this production did not belong to them. They were given only the gross and misleading figures. Yet, even a small share of the quoted figures represented heavy income for the nation – for as long as it continued. Few Australians stopped to worry how long the exports of minerals would continue to support them in the manner to which they had become accustomed. As long as those

Americans dug the stuff out and those Japanese continued to buy it everything would be all right, mate. But for how long?

Dr B. M. Oliver, Vice President for research and development of the Californian firm, Hewlett-Packard, warned in Melbourne that unless there was a conversion to nuclear power at once the next generation would literally run out of gas. He said that if the entire world enjoyed the same standard of living as the average American, existing supplies of chromium would last a mere 45 years, nickel would run out in 25 years, tungsten in 13 years, copper in 12 years, lead in 11 years, zinc and tin in 9 years, molybdenum in 8 years, mercury in 4 years and silver in only 1 year.

The knowledge that traditional sources of power were also going to run short soon had prompted the United States to take preliminary steps to ensure that the turbines and furnaces of the world did not come to a stop. The U.S. government had arranged in 1971 discussions with Australia, Canada, Japan, the United Kingdom and the European Economic Community for the construction of uranium enrichment plants on a multi-national basis. Australia, with its large reserves of uranium – despite the Queensland Mines fiasco – and its other natural resources, offered the best prospects for the establishment of a plant to supply the Pacific and South East Asian Zone.

Now the Americans had a real vested interest in what happened in Australia. According to a U.S. Treasury White Paper, American company investment in Australia in mid-1971 was running at something close to $US 3.2 billion. This represented America's fourth largest investment overseas. 500 subsidiaries of American firms were in Australia and another 1,400 firms in Australia had licence arrangements with American firms.

It was amusing that while some Australians were strongly opposed to U.S. investment in Australia they were unaware that U.S. labour organizations were even more bitterly against it. The American unions had become worried about the unemployment problem in the United

States, and took the view that every American company established in a foreign country robbed the U.S. of job vacancies. America's major foreign-trade organization, the National Foreign Trade Council, was anxious to refute this. After a survey of U.S. foreign traders and investors it reported that there was no evidence to support the allegation that offshore-U.S. production had reduced American exports and domestic employment in the companies investing abroad. The Council was concerned about legislation introduced in the U.S. Congress which would alter the tax income from foreign affiliates with the intention of removing the existing tax incentives and imposing new taxes on royalty income. The proposed new legislation would also impose new controls over the outflow of capital for foreign direct investment and would impose controls over the outflow of technology. It would also establish a new agency to impose quotas on imports to achieve so-called industrial self-sufficiency within the U.S. and would affirm the purpose of insuring that the production of goods which historically had been produced in the United States would be continued and maintained.

The National Foreign Trade Council said that companies it had surveyed had stressed that their marketing positions had been strengthened and their sales had grown substantially around the world as a result of their investments abroad. U.S. labour had been producing equipment which some of the companies had been installing in their overseas plants. Furthermore foreign production was mostly for sale within the country of manufacture. The Council also contended that imports from foreign affiliates were still negligible, and that technology transferred to foreign affiliates of U.S. companies was considered to be most highly advanced only in one or two cases.

Australia could not have had a better lobbyist in Washington than the National Foreign Trade Council in the view of those in favour of U.S. investment in Australia. On the other hand there were Australians who fervently hoped that the American unions would prevail.

14
Trade

The American government headed the most ferociously competitive free-enterprise people in the world. They were a people accustomed to commercial cannibalism in which the strong were always ready to gobble up the weak. The policies of the U.S. government were often based upon the need to placate these cannibals, and this need frequently had priority over almost all outside considerations.

Too often the Australian government had shown that it did not understand the priorities and difficulties of the U.S. government. The Australians seemed forever hopeful of uncovering a soft under-belly of sentiment in Washington relating to Australian trade – an attitude contrary to hard-headed realism. They assumed that the U.S. government would be prepared to offer favours to a faithful ally – to good old Australia, the kinfolk country – even if U.S. businessmen and unionists and lobbyists did squeal about it. The Australians were often painfully surprised when the limp but friendly hand they extended to Washington was savaged between sharp teeth.

Assumptions that Australia was entitled to favoured treatment had grown in the hot-house climate of preferences and protection from Britain and had survived far too long.

In 1967 Prime Minister Harold Holt of Australia interceded personally with President Johnson and Secretary of State Dean Rusk to get a better trade deal. Holt thought that by walking through Washington and by calling out at intervals that he was all the way with L.B.J. he would win so many friends that the U.S. government would remove its tariff barrier against Australian wool. Holt's impact upon the United States government was like that of oxygen – enlivening, but colourless and elementary and soon dispersed. The U.S. government was committed to stand by its own wool growers and in no way intended to alter that policy. All that happened as a result of Holt's visit was that President Johnson ordered another cordial but pointless round of discussions between Australian and American trade officials to enable Holt to go home saying that he had achieved something when in truth he had achieved nothing whatever. The second round of trade talks followed exactly the same futile lines as the first. The trade boys knew that they would have been wasting less time had they been playing pool together or had they been having contests in Indian wrestling.

There followed two Australian reactions. The more immediate was an emotional outburst from the leader of the Australian Country Party, John McEwen, which had a familiar Australian whine about it: 'Australia has every right to expect the U.S. to reduce the wool tariff. We are one of her principal friends and wool is our principal export-earner. Australia is one of America's best customers for her exports. We buy twice as much from the U.S. as she buys from us. Only five per cent of Australian wool goes to America – and America is the only major market with more than a nominal tariff on its import.'

The other reaction was rougher. It was launched on 19 May 1971 by a member of the Australian Wool Board, Mr G. Chance, who claimed that tariffs imposed during the 1930s to protect the American woolgrowers and textile manufacturers were now costing the Australian woolgrowers at least $70 million a year. Moreover the U.S. tariffs had not achieved their purpose. Instead of protecting the manufacturers of wool textiles in America they had encouraged them to use man-made fibres instead of wool. Mr Chance recklessly advocated a counter attack against the United States, along the line of that made in 1934. He thought that the Australian government should impose tariffs on all synthetic fibre products of American origin entering

Australia or being manufactured in Australia under licence, and to use the funds gained to subsidize Australian woolgrowers. Chance accused the American government of damaging the Australian wool industry to subsidize its own wretchedly inefficient wool industry. He said that the American tariff amounted to about 45 per cent of the clean price of Australian broad and medium wools. He claimed that about 70 per cent of the raw wool tariffs collected on Australian wool was used by the American government to prop up American sheepmen. The American wool producers were receiving about 33 cents a pound in subsidies for all the wool they produced so that their total return per pound, including other forms of price support, was around 90 cents (U.S.). The total U.S. subsidy of 33 cents was more than some Australian woolmen had been getting in total prices for their vastly superior wool.

Chance added: 'The ridiculous aspect of the situation is that American woolgrowers still cannot produce wool economically and are rapidly declining in number. American wool production has dropped from about 450 million pounds in 1942 to less than 200 million pounds in 1969. The accumulated funds from the tariffs which are used to subsidize American producers amount to about $US540 million. Therefore, if tariffs were abolished immediately this amount would be adequate to pay the 33 cents subsidy to every American woolgrower for the next nine years.' Chance asserted that Australia also was being indirectly victimized by U.S. tariffs on imports of manufactured wool products. These tariffs were a serious threat to the Japanese wool textile industry which was the biggest buyer of Australian wool. The tariffs had been intended to protect American wool textile manufacturers but their result had been to force wool prices beyond the reach of these manufacturers, compelling them in turn to use increasing amounts of man-made fibres. This meant that the vast sums of money being spent on wool promotion in the United States by the International Wool Secretariat were being negated because of the almost impossible situation in which wool had to compete against synthetics. Chance was convinced that he knew the score.

Australian heat on the subject of wool tariffs was understandable. Wool had been the firm base of the Australian economy. In 1966 Australian wool had been selling at international auctions at up to $2 per pound. Every Australian sheepman had been rolling in money and some had celebrated the end of wool sales in Australian cities with wild grog and girl parties and with cossack dancing on hotel tables. But by the end of 1971 the price of the same type of wool had dropped to below 30 cents a pound, and many of the same sheepmen had empty pockets and the backside out of their pants. Stud merino rams of the type that had been worth thousands of dollars each in 1966 were being sold in 1971 in Sydney for pet food. Other stud rams were being virtually smuggled out of Australia for sale to foreign sheepmen in disregard of trade union leaders who believed that such sales would ultimately make the quality of foreign-produced wool much better.

In May 1971 the U.S. government became annoyed over a multi-million dollar deal between an Australian-Canadian machinery firm, Massey-Ferguson Holdings, and Cuba. The Australian company had contracted to sell sugar cane harvesting machines to the communist island. The Australian government shrugged off the Americans' disapproval – but was soon reminded that the Australian Sugar Board was at that time in Washington trying to preserve the Australian share in the U.S. sugar market worth some $20 million annually.

Another disagreement occurred over airline flights across the Pacific. Pan American Airways and American Airlines demanded additional flights for their aircraft but were opposed by Qantas, owned by the Australian government. In retaliation a U.S. threat was made to deny Qantas landing rights in the United States. The Australian government capitulated with ill-grace.

For many years Qantas had done its best to fight

off the inroads of foreign competition along its routes while at the same time keeping its air fares high. Suddenly it found itself losing business to charter flight airlines which offered substantially cheaper fares out of international airports such as Singapore. One charter group, the American outfit, World Airways, began lobbying in Canberra for permission to operate fifty charter flights from the United States to Australia in 1973 carrying about 10,000 American tourists. World Airways made it known that these tourists would spend at least $5 million when they reached Australia. The Australian tourist industry cheered, but not the Qantas organization. By the beginning of 1972 Qantas had tightened its economy but had fired many of its young pilots and aircrew trainees. It looked like the beginning of just another American takeover in Australia. However, Qantas began moving with the times and in a surprising fight-back drastically reduced some of its air fares, driving the ball back into its competitors' court and upsetting international air fare agreements.

From New York a newspaper correspondent advised Australians that if they hung on long enough they might yet obtain a better deal from General Dynamics over the unsatisfactory purchase of F111 aircraft. The Australian government had refused to accept the planes until faults had been rectified, and the twenty-four aircraft costing $300 million had been parked out in the open at Fort Worth, Texas, for more than a year like junk jallopies on a used car lot. Not even the fame and popularity of the former Davis Cup tennis player, Ted Schroeder – whom General Dynamics had shrewdly appointed as their Australian representative – was able to sweeten the situation.

There was no doubt that when the Australian government dropped its milksop expectations of favouritism and got down to hard bargaining in trade on valid commercial grounds it did better. And if Australia's businessmen ever found that they had a well-led and gutsy government behind them – co-operating and planning with them and fighting for them all the way down the line as the

American and Japanese governments did for their businessmen – they would begin to have more wins than losses. A team effort always did beat solo performances in trade.

As a trading nation Australia had been feeling the growing chill of geographical isolation from Britain but her other outlets for her exports had been changing dramatically. In 1937-8 Britain took 54.8 per cent of Australia's exports while the United States had taken only 6.9 per cent. By 1970-1 Britain was headed into the European Economic Community and was taking only 11.2 per cent of Australia's exports. However, by then the United States was taking 11.9 per cent. Only six months later the trend had moved much further with Britain buying only 8.3 per cent over the period and the United States buying 13.7 per cent. By then Japan had become Australia's best customer buying almost twice as much from her than did the Americans.

The U.S. purchases from Australia concentrated mainly on beef exports with purchases of sugar, iron ore and other minerals of much smaller values. But it was sometimes pointed out that the backbone of Australia's foreign earnings was the market in Japan for the minerals which Americans had played such a leading role in developing. The U.S. ambassador to Australia, Mr Rice, also reminded Australians in 1971 that the U.S. had become an important indirect market for Australian exports because it bought finished goods from Japan which in turn used raw materials purchased from Australia. This did not ease the anxiety felt at the Department of Trade in Canberra. Australia remained extremely vulnerable as a world trader. Other nations could form comfortable trading blocs with their neighbours, but without the goodwill of the United States and Japan – her principal customers – and without their continued prosperity – Australia would be left out on a limb and could fall into serious economic trouble.

From time to time the United States government tried to make Australians believe that they were not doing too badly. It explained that in the instance of sugar America had transferred its purchases from Cuba to less developed countries which badly needed a helping hand, such as the Philippines, Puerto Rico and the Virgin Islands. But Australia, which could hardly be classified as poverty-stricken, had also been given a share of the U.S. sugar market. Indeed, some members of the U.S. Congress had objected, claiming that a sugar quota for Australia would be a subsidy since the American price for sugar brought in under the quota system was about double the world price. Australia had the largest U.S. sugar quota of any developed country in the world, and had the additional prospect of sharing in any short-fall of sugar shipped to the U.S. by other countries.

When it came to U.S. imports of beef, veal and mutton Australia was again doing rather well by comparison with other nations. Eleven countries participated in the U.S. allocations but Australia had captured a quota of about 50 per cent of the total U.S. imports of meat. In fact 62 per cent of all of Australia's exports of beef and veal was exported to the United States. This meat had sold at prices averaging 65 per cent more for mutton and 23 per cent more for beef above the prices paid to Australia by Britain. The U.S. government pointed out that if it had lifted restrictions on meat imports the price levels would have deteriorated. (And of course, Australian beef would still have undersold American-grown beef.)

Despite all assurances, the Australian economy trembled when the worst happened and a trading war between Japan and the United States boiled over during 1971. A bill went before the U.S. House of Representatives authorizing quotas on any foreign product that won as much as 15 per cent of the U.S. market, with the chief target being Japan. The Australian government stood dumbly on the sidelines watching the conflict worsen between her two major trading partners. The unyielding attitudes of both the U.S. and Japan were dictated by insular political considerations and domestic problems, but the outcome of their dispute could become a serious economic blow to other countries, particularly Australia. The Australian government should not have been content to permit a trade dispute of possibly dire consequences remain merely a two-way discussion. Any initiative by Australia to act as an intermediary between the two countries could have been extremely useful for all concerned. It would have served to remind the two great nations of the vital needs and interests of other smaller nations within the Pacific and South East Asia trading area. It could have outlined the framework for a new Pacific and South East Asia Trade and Development Area – an essential form of regionalism for smaller and less developed countries in the area, and of potentially great importance in world trade.

The seriousness of the situation was underlined by the fact that in 1971 Japan had been taking 93 per cent of Australian coal exports, 88 per cent of her iron exports and 57 per cent of her aluminium exports. Minerals exported in unprocessed form to Japan made a vital contribution to Australia's export earnings and plugged the gaping hole in foreign earnings caused by the decline of the wool industry. Nationalists might complain about foreigners controlling Australia's mineral deposits, but the nation's minority share of the proceeds had been keeping the economy afloat. So true had this become that Australia was now far too dependent upon those sales to Japan. It followed that when the U.S. stamped upon Japan's trading foot, Australia also felt pain and yelped like a pup.

In August 1971 President Nixon's decision to impose a 10 per cent surcharge on general imports into the United States, plus an accompanying international monetary crisis, worsened a recession in Japan and helped to start one in Australia. The Japanese cut, cancelled, or postponed orders of Australian minerals because production in their secondary industries and their own exports had fallen.

Ironically, in Australia, the biggest companies hit by the easing of the Japanese market were American-owned or had substantial American interests. They had to put some of their huge development projects into moth balls until good times returned.

Some Americans in Australia were almost as dismayed by the abrasive behaviour of the U.S. government trade officials who had jackbooted their way into Japan, Hong Kong and other countries to dictate the terms of the hard new American trade policies. They had over-reacted from being suckers to the other extreme of being insulting and overbearing. One British official in Hong Kong had complained that he had never been spoken to so rudely before. The affronted Japanese had smiled politely under similar treatment and had hissed softly between their teeth and bowed – but they would not forget or forgive easily. U.S. goodwill in the Far East had become non-existent, and would take a long time to recover.

Steps to evaluate Australia were taken in 1971 when she was invited to become a member of the Organization for Economic Co-operation and Development. O.E.C.D. was an exclusive club of nations. The original membership had been limited to the eighteen countries which had been members of the Organization for European Economic Co-operation during the rebuilding of postwar Europe – plus Canada and the United States. Since 1961 only three other nations had been invited to join. They had been Japan, Switzerland, and now Australia.

The aims of O.E.C.D. were to achieve the highest sustainable economic growth and employment and a rising standard of living in member countries while maintaining financial stability and thus contributing to the development of the world economy. Its charter also nobly vowed to contribute to sound economic expansion in member and non-member countries in the process of economic development.

Membership of O.E.C.D. promised to end Australia's long isolation from the major economic forums of the western world. It could give Australia the double benefits of expert advice and planning on an international scale.

Henceforth bush politicians and self-taught economists in Canberra would have fewer opportunities to dissipate their country's wealth in either coldly calculated political stunts or in parliamentary blunders resulting from ignorance and prejudice. It would both assist and restrain the expert advisers to the Australian government within the Public Service in Canberra. In short O.E.C.D. could mean the beginning of a far better system of planning in Australia and the basis of a sounder and more orderly development – and which could become of considerable importance to Washington and to U.S. investors.

The island chain of nations which Japan had set out to conquer in the Second World War formed a natural trading region of potential strength. However, for thirty years up to 1972 Australia's trade with her island neighbours had been both small and static. On the last available figures up to 1972 Australia's exports to the Philippines, Indonesia, the Pacific islands and New Zealand – plus exports to the giant populations of India and Pakistan – had amounted to only 21 per cent of her total exports. Imports into Australia from all those countries annually added up to only about 9 per cent of total imports. People in Canberra who knew this were apt to shrug because they knew the main reason for it and thought it to be beyond remedy. The industries of most of Australia's neighbour countries were so undeveloped or primitive that they produced little that Australians wished to buy. The neighbour countries, on the other hand, had a huge total population but could not buy Australian products in great amounts because they were too poor.

Obviously something needed to be done about it. Time would bring many changes but there was a danger that they would not be changes satisfactory to Australia or to the United States. The peoples of the region would not remain for ever satisfied or indifferent to slow social and economic progress, nor were they likely to be politically quiet or unaware of world events. The United States needed to attend to the problem if it believed that the best interests of America's global defence strategy would be served by having a free and prosperous community of nations in the Australian region. Procrastination by the U.S. government could result in some of these countries falling into economic or military bondage to other great world powers.

Large amounts of assistance would be needed in training, equipment and technology and it would be beyond Australia's capacity to play anything but a minor role. The United States would have to accept a large part of the task if it were to succeed. However, it lay easily within the capacity of America – and would be a much more successful and more rewarding foreign venture than becoming involved in wars on the Asian mainland. Businesmen from the United States, Japan, Britain, and Australia could see the future of the region clearly. One group of Australian businessmen, backed for once by the Australian Government, announced plans in 1971 to launch a feasibility study for the establishment of a major industrial complex in southern Java. A multi-million dollar scheme was planned around the port of Tjilatjap and included plans for an oil refinery and a steelworks. The steelworks possibly would use Australian iron ore and natural gas from a new field in Indonesia. The establishment of an industrial estate beside the port was envisaged. A consortium based in Perth, the Australian-Indonesian Manufacturing and Trade Operations Company, had financed the feasibility study and was the driving power behind it.

Comalco, based in Australia, but with its international financing, was also looking towards Indonesia. In 1972 the company took 45 per cent of the shares in a joint venture with Indonesian and Hong Kong partners to manufacture and market aluminium products there. Dowell Australia Limited took a 60 per cent interest in Papua New Guinea's biggest aluminium fabricator and glass distributor, Territory Glass and Aluminium Pty Limited. The restless Japanese had their business prospectors and investors frequently visiting all the countries north of Australia looking for profitable new industrial projects.

Meanwhile U.S. businessmen, always on the ball, had seen the strategic advantages of Australia as a head-quarters and anchor country for business expansion to the surrounding region and beyond it. Among the first American companies to establish regional offices in Australia had been General Motors-Holden's and Ford. By mid-1972 more than eighty other big American companies had based their regional offices in Australia. On 1 January 1972, the cigarette group, Philip Morris, moved its Asia-Pacific operations from New York to Melbourne. Its objectives were to exploit the immense export opportunities north from Australia – in Indonesia, the Philippines, Malaysia and Japan, and later India. Perhaps even China one day. A company spokesman commented: 'We are going closer to where all the people are.' In fact what the company had decided to do was to take advantage of the shorter lines of transportation and communications available from Australia – the same advantages which had so greatly helped General MacArthur in war-time.

15

The last option

The Australian government was not prepared for America's sudden decision in late 1971 to seek a better understanding with Communist China. So faithfully had it been following the U.S. official policy of total opposition to Communist China that it was not able to alter course quickly enough to keep in line with the latest U.S. move. Canberra was continuing to make statements according to the old policy almost right up to the moment that Washington announced the new one. It would have highlighted Australia's resemblance to an undignified American-satellite administration had not the governments of Japan and other Pacific countries shared Canberra's acute embarrassment, shock and anger. President Nixon had not taken any of them into his confidence either.

The twists and turns of foreign policies and alliances in the need to maintain the balance of world power do not surprise students of history, but people and their governments are seldom able to take a detached long-range view of their own times as being history in the making. The re-emergence in current affairs of a recognizable historic pattern usually catches them off guard as being something entirely new and unexpected. So it was with the impact of America's buddy effort towards China. People found difficulty in believing it after the twenty years of mud-slinging between the two countries.

It was a political blow below the belt for Prime Minister McMahon of Australia. He had been vigorously countering the Australian Labor Party's campaign for closer links between Australia and Communist China. In fact the Leader of the A.L.P., Gough Whitlam had just returned from a visit to Peking which had earned him some fleeting fame as a latter-day Marco Polo. McMahon had been doing his utmost to counter and belittle Whitlam's efforts and policies – and right at that crucial moment in Australian politics President Nixon had demonstrated that Whitlam had been on the right track. Prime Minister McMahon had been left with egg all over his face. Justifiably, the Australian government felt slighted and annoyed. Even a few days warning from Washington would have enabled McMahon to have taken some initiative to soften the impact. There was a hot line between Washington and Canberra, but the U.S. administration seemed to have forgotten about it. The omission was seen as another unfortunate indication of the insignificance of Australia in calculations in Washington.

A second point about the change in American policy that wounded the Australian government was that it had been made with the same lack of consideration for Australia that the U.S. had reserved for Japan. The Australians believed themselves to be a close friend of the U.S. – whereas there had been a growing coolness between the U.S. and Japan. This coolness in fact had been one of the reasons for the American change in policy towards China. The U.S. had become convinced that the crafty Japanese had been playing America for a sucker. The crutch of American aid and generosity which the Japanese nation had needed so desperately after its devastating defeat in the Second World War had been retained long after the Japanese could no longer pretend that they were still limping. Modern Japan had become much too hale and hearty, too rich and ambitious at America's expense.

One of the reasons for Japan's prosperity had been that she had relied almost solely on the U.S. for defence under the excuse that her Constitution forbade any military expenditure on a large scale. Furthermore it had become evident that Japan had become too tough in other directions – ready to accept aid and preferences from the

U.S. but not willing to extend generosity and aid to under-developed Asian neighbours. And there had been serious trade difficulties developing between the two countries.

The re-emergence of the historic pattern of the 1930s was discernible. Forty years earlier the U.S. had been opposed to Japan economically and racially and had been becoming wary of her future territorial ambitions and military intentions. In the mid-1930s the U.S. had been displaying a sympathy and liking for the Chinese. Now, in the 1970s some Americans were saying openly that they preferred Communist China to democratic Japan.

Prime Minister Sato of Japan personally compared the American change of policy with the treacherous Hitler-Stalin Pact of 1939. At that time Japan had an alliance with Germany directed against the Soviet Union, but without warning Germany had begun conferring with Russia about mutual spheres of interest, and leaving Japan out of it. In 1971, in Sato's opinion, the United States was becoming comparable to Nazi Germany while China had replaced Russia as Japan's main danger.

The possible repercussions from the American change of foreign policy caused genuine alarm in the Department of Foreign Affairs in Canberra. Any injury or slight to a proud and potentially powerful Japan was risky. Any shift in world alliances which left Japan feeling excluded and double-crossed was perilous. Outside the Department of Foreign Affairs many other Australians had not forgotten nor forgiven the barbarisms of Japan in the Second World War, and had been sure that militarism would re-emerge in Japan one day – and now they worried that a reconciliation between the United States and China could trigger it off. They saw a distinct possibility that such a reconciliation would throw Japan and Russia closer together, the final move in the adjusting of balances, but not a welcome one.

A monthly review by Britain's Barclay's Bank in 1971 had commented that economically Japan and Australia were natural partners. That was all right as long as it was a partnership of equality, but Australians could not overlook Japan's most pressing problems – massive industrialization but few natural resources; a densely crowded population but not much land. With such pressures inside Japan Australians did not feel too safe being described as her natural economic partner. They felt even less safe at the prospect of a resurgent Japan which had been aroused by American moves in the power game. The Philippine government called a regional conference to consider the U.S. approach to China. Korea, Thailand, South Vietnam, Malaysia, Singapore, Indonesia, New Zealand, Japan and Australia were invited to send delegates. Nothing much came of it.

In November 1971, Prime Minister McMahon made a pilgrimage to Washington as all Australian prime ministers had done since the Second World War and the decline of British power. It was important and necessary that Australia's leaders should represent their country occasionally in Washington. However, such visits, together with most references to defence problems, had become debased in Australia through having been used too many times for party political propaganda. There had been too many attempts to use such journeys to Washington to divert public attention from the deficiencies of government at home. Part of the political ploy was to be photographed with the arm of the American President about one's shoulders. Vague American assurances and half-promises could easily be extracted and publicized and it did not matter if all of these were forgotten within three months.

McMahon, on his visit, did nothing out of the ordinary. He renewed suggestions that the nebulous naval base at Cockburn Sound on the Australian west coast could become a suitable replacement for Singapore and an ideal pivot for defence by the U.S. and Australia and the British against both Russian and Asian military expansion in the future. His staff organized an excellent news and television coverage of his meeting with President Nixon which was promptly relayed to impress the Australian public; and the President obliged by uttering the expected platitudes about American-Australian friendship. To make damn sure that his visit to the White House would not go unrecorded in the American Press, McMahon instructed his wife to wear a spectacular gown split from ankle to hip on either side, in which she visited the White House and shocked the society prudes.

It was not really McMahon's fault that the routine political stage-managing did not succeed at home. He had done his best but the Australian public would have preferred his visit to have been a low-key business journey instead of a public relations expedition. They could no longer be convinced that a trip to the United States and a talk with the President by their Prime Minister was the pinnacle of genuine leadership. They wanted some solid performances in future for the expenditure of taxpayers' money, and less political showmanship. But it was unfair to write McMahon off too early.

Soon after the Washington visit the U.S. Under Secretary for Defence, Packard, went to Australia. Packard, who was within only a few weeks of his resignation, was in favour of closing down many of the U.S. bases overseas to save money. He told an Australian Press Conference that the Nixon doctrine expected other countries to bear a larger amount of the security responsibility for their own particular areas of the world. Therefore he did not see any likelihood that U.S. forces would be stationed in Australia in the near future. It was clearly Australia's responsibility to provide leadership for its own part of the world. But then Packard revealed that the U.S. government was considering whether it should provide the necessary technology to help Australia to build up her own defences.

The Australian Press let this last remark pass almost unrecorded. It could have been the most important outcome of McMahon's visit to Washington. Modern technological knowledge was what Australia needed most to enable her to establish defence industries so that she could become more self-reliant. It was no longer in America's best interests to regard Australia as being simply a good customer for the U.S. defence industries, nor could the U.S. government wisely afford to have the Australians alternating between periods of free-loading or non-expenditure on defence and *ad hoc* purchases of armaments for political propaganda to win elections. Disregarding the too-often repeated cry of wolf from the Australians to incite either Britain or the U.S. to build a permanent shield for them, the U.S. had to see the danger in the changing balance of power.

The dismemberment of the old British Empire had left many new trading opportunities and strategic vacancies around the world. The smaller countries had not been able to take full advantage of these. As always the bigger powers had benefited most. Japan for example, had concentrated on replacing British trade supremacy with her own in former Empire countries, including Australia. More ominously the Soviet Union had been attracted by the military opportunities opened to her by Britain's withdrawal and contraction. Russia had built up her naval and merchant fleets, had become a major sea power and had sought a global pre-eminence as once Britain had done. Furthermore Russia had been following the same path to empire that Britain had taken centuries earlier. The Russians had moved down into the Mediterranean and had become firmly based and entrenched in Egypt. Had it not been for the Israelis the Russians would have had the Suez Canal long since. Even without the canal the Russians had established refuelling bases for their ships in the Indian Ocean. They now operated out of the former British fuelling base at Mauritius, and had gained an air base in the former British colony of Ceylon. Not only had they gained a foothold in South East Asia but they also had become the patron of India as Britain once had been. The Russian backing of the Indians in the war with Pakistan in 1971 had sealed her future influence in that sub-continent ... And all this

Russian progress had been achieved while the United
States had been bogged down in Indo-China for nine
wasted years of ruinous warfare.

The Australian region therefore remained one of the
few options left to the United States to take up a care-
taker and development role in what remained of the
former British possessions. The Australian continent,
which had been one of the most valuable portions of the
British Empire, remained one of the few areas where
the United States could move in peacefully to adjust
the balance of power against the Soviet Union.

Most Australians acknowledge that they are a multi-
racial nation – they seldom really think about it any
more. Permanent residents of Australia, in addition to
the Aborigines, include people from all parts of Europe,
and from Asia and North and South America. Every year
10,000 non-Caucasians and people of mixed blood are
permitted to settle in Australia. Many more Asians enter
Australia illegally, some of them being smuggled ashore
at points along the desolate stretches of coastline and
being hidden in the cities until their friends or relatives
think that they can fend for themselves or until their
employers have a sheltered job for them. As long as
they stay out of the way of the police and do not attract
attention to themselves they do not have to worry much
about being picked up for breaking immigration laws.
Chinese restaurants in Australia are full of Chinese
waiters, for example, who were supposedly born in Australia, but who strangely have never learned English.

Increasing trade with other nations of the South Pacific
and the South East Asian region must mean that in
the future Indonesians, Japanese, Melanesians from New
Guinea and Papua, and Polynesians will be settling in
Australia. Torres Strait Islanders, black-skinned descendants of warlike, seagoing tribes, already live in northern
Australia. It has been impossible to keep them out. The
ignoramuses and the fashionable and often hypocritical
people who want an end to the once absurdly named
White Australia immigration policy will see their wish

come true soon enough. The future problem is going to lie in preventing racial blocs and hatreds from developing as in America.

Australian governments were always sensitive to the disadvantages and dangers of a multi-racial society. Australians used to detest the 'Balts' and Italian migrants and the Maltese and were not too keen on the Greeks either. Turkish migrants fell into disfavour in Australia because their native culture and religion tended to segregate them from the rest of the community, and their habit of slaughtering sheep in the backyard or the kitchen of their homes did not fit well into the customs of Australian suburbia. Nothing was more certain than the fact that the last people that Australians wanted as migrants were American negroes. The impact of negro violence in the United States had been too great upon Australia to make them acceptable. No doubt this was an injustice to millions of peaceful and decent-living American negroes and to those who believed themselves to be fighting for equality, justice and human dignity in a former slave country – but feeling in Australia was strongly anti-negro-immigration. This has continued and could yet cause conflict in future relations between Australia and the United States.

American negroes who have applied to Australian authorities for permission to migrate to Australia have not been encouraged to return for a second interview. A few with outstanding qualifications in science or in some other highly specialized field of occupation have stood a chance of getting into Australia – but only about one chance in a million. No reasons have ever been given to those negroes wanting to migrate to Australia who have been rejected. At the beginning of 1972 there were fewer than a dozen negroes living permanently in Australia. Three of them were residing in the State of Victoria. Any negro who tries to enter Australia illegally seems to be much more quickly detected than an illegal Asian migrant, and invariably is deported.

It has become a continuing policy of Australian governments not to import America's racial problems. This effectively prevented Australia from conducting an active migrant recruitment campaign in the U.S. Australian governments were afraid that the 'wrong' people might apply and that would be an embarrassment all round. Therefore, the Australian attempt to attract white Americans into emigrating was always a delicate, cautious, and almost overt procedure like trying to steal the plums out of someone else's pudding. It consisted mainly of planting in American newspapers 'success' stories about local people who had already become migrants and who had made good in Australia. They did not include stories about blacks in Australia.

A gallup poll was not required to conclude that the majority of Australians in the early 1970s would have been whole-heartedly in sympathy with the views expressed in 1751 by Benjamin Franklin when he objected to what he described bluntly as the 'blackening' of America. Franklin asked 'Why increase the sons of Africa by planting them in America where we have so fair an opportunity ...?' Franklin was a racist, but Australians knew that millions of present-day Americans wished fervently that the government of his time had heeded his advice.

On several occasions after 1970 the British Racial Relations Board chided the Australian government for not granting assisted ship passages to enable coloured people to migrate from England to Australia. A large-scale migration of such people from Britain to Australia would, of course, have well suited the British government. In a fit of sentimentality during the dismantling of the Empire the British had permitted hundreds of thousands of West Indian negroes, Indians, and Pakistanis to flock into England as migrants, and had suffered racial indigestion ever since. The Australians did not wish this to happen to their country if they could avoid it.

The Australian Government always responded to the British Racial Relations Board with dignity, but if it had chosen to be unpleasant it could have reminded the board of the era when Bristol and Liverpool were two of the world's principal slaving ports. During the 18th century the British slave trade to America transformed Liverpool from a fishing village of only 5,000 inhabitants into a great city. In the year of 1752 alone eighty-eight Liverpool vessels carried almost 25,000 negro slaves from Africa to the West Indies, from whence many of them were re-exported to the American mainland. By 1774 half of Liverpool's sailors were engaged in the black slave trade. It was a common saying that Liverpool's principal streets were marked out by slave chains and the walls of its houses were cemented by the blood of the Africans.

In the majority, Australians believe that Britain's negroes should remain Britain's sole responsibility. Similarly they believe that the negroes of the United States should remain the responsibility of America, particularly those who carry their own 'Hate-Whitey' racist chip on their shoulders. It is always possible that Australians might one day be persuaded to relent and experiment with a more generous relaxation of their immigration laws, but they know well that unfortunate results from such experiments are not reversible. Most Australians do not believe the risk should be taken – despite the differing view of some important people such as the Labor leader, Gough Whitlam.

Will Australia ever become another United States as George Train, Mark Twain, King O'Malley and other Americans hoped? Nowadays most Australians would hope not. They want to succeed where Americans have failed. They wish to remain a happier nation and a healthier one.

Television has given Australians a one-sided image of American ugliness, just as the old Hollywood movies used to present the opposite extreme. Australians have been appalled by the American drug and crime problem and disintegration of civilized society as presented on television. This dismaying image has been supported by reports from homecoming Australians who express their abhorrence of the violence and shambles of big American cities. They strengthen the determination of Australians not to catch the 'U.S. sickness'. They worsen the fear of other Australians that their country will catch it. Most assuredly Australians no longer experience that old sense of inferiority they used to have towards the United States nor the envy. They like the fine types of Americans who predominate among those who have gone to Australia. They cannot understand how such courteous and civilized people, who blend into their community like Cousin George or Aunt Ethel, could be representatives of a country which has taken such a down-turn. They feel sorry for them and disappointed in the United States Yet it seems that the future of Australia and the United States must continue to be closely linked, and that U.S. influence in Australia will continue to be profound.

An American historian, Professor Hartly Grattan, of the University of Texas, saw the problem during a visit to Sydney and urged Australians to be more careful about what they were prepared to accept from America during the 1970s. 'Don't take what comes your way from the United States because you feel a security dependence on the United States or an economic dependence on the United States,' he warned. 'All kinds of influences on you will flow out of America and some of them will be bad. I don't think Australia is at present sufficiently critical of the United States.'

I believe that Australians have become critical of the United States, and it is a good thing for both countries that this has happened.

16

Americanization

The Americanization of Australia, which took root
through the influence of Hollywood in the 1930s, and
sprouted during the Second World War, has grown
robustly. It has invaded almost every aspect of Australian
life. Even the most British of Australians have become
accustomed to it.

At the Gold Coast, Queensland's flashy seaside resort,
people basking in the sunshine could wonder what country they are in for all around them are beaches or
motels called 'Miami' or 'Florida Gardens', 'Pasadena' or
the 'El Paso'. The U.S. yacht *American Eagle*, races for
line honours in the Sydney to Hobart race. The champion
racehorse, *Igloo*, breaks down in Perth, and its trainer
breaks the bad news to its American owner, Mrs M. E.
Tippett. The American golfers, Jack Nicklaus, Lee Tre-
vino and Arnold Palmer have regularly made it tough
for other competitors on the Australian circuit. American
school children are in Australian schools on exchange
visits, and the Aussie kids who went to the U.S. come
back home one year later with American accents you
could cut with a knife. Australian nurses and doctors
disappear across the Pacific to earn more money in
America. Economic consultants, Harris, Kerr and Forster
of Los Angeles advise the Australian Government how
to make more revenue out of Ayers Rock and American
tourists. A fan of Elvis Presley, Mrs Ellen French of
Sydney, sends $20 to another fan, Mrs Lucy Hottens-
dein of Salt Lake City, so that she can attend a Presley
concert on her 100th birthday. Management consultants,
McKinsey and Company of New York helped the Australian Liberal Party to plan its 1972 election campaign

'out of friendship for all Australians.' The Australian newspapers are full of such stuff.

Australian management in offices and factories have adopted American management techniques and procedures as their own. Inside most shops American merchandising methods are used, and on their selling counters is the evidence of American-style packaging and presentation of goods. American-style advertising helps to sell them, and the Australian advertising agencies which are still not owned by American companies shamelessly riffle through every U.S. newspaper and magazine to steal every new American advertising gimmick shortly after every new one appears.

In the streets the catch-cries of Australian students, dropouts, hippies and demonstrators, their living habits and apparel, and often their causes and thoughts are aped from their peers in America. The generation gap and student action and freak-outs and pot have been gas importations, man – and so too have been Indian beads, flower power and that dear old stage show *Hair*, fringed buckskin jackets and black leather motor cycle jackets with 'Hell's Angels' stencilled across the shoulder blades. It has been this way in Australia since the times of Davey Crockett fur hats, bobby socks and Frank Sinatra's personal appearances and way before that.

The Australian language is studded with American words and phrases. When 'containerization', 'this particular point in time', or 'meaningful dialogue' first cropped up in New York or Washington or Frisco, only a few days passed before they were being parroted in Sydney, Canberra, or Adelaide.

Something that intrigues and amuses American visitors is the widespread usage in Australia of archaic, moss-covered American slang. Colloquial expressions or cute phrasing from the U.S. movies, television, pop music or from the mouths of visiting American personalities, stick in the Australian language like flies in ice cream. They remain alive there long after they have become dated and killed off in their place of origin. It is understandable that borrowed slang remains unchanged. Australian colloquialisms evolve and die just as rapidly as do the American variety in their native domain. But it still surprises that the Australian language is a museum of U.S. slang.

Colonel Sanders finger-lickin' good fried chicken stalls have become firmly established in every city and in most big country towns of Australia. It is a symptom of changing Australian eating habits and food tastes. Beef, veal and mutton consumption in Australia is down from 201 pounds per head in 1939 to 121 pounds in the 1970s, a 40 per cent reduction. However, the frozen food industry which has been doggedly following American developments has been resisted by Australians who claim that snap-freezing ruins flavour. Luckily for them they still have the greatest choice of food, frozen or fresh, of perhaps any people on earth.

The Australians were informed in July 1971 by Mr F. M. Legge, the U.S. Agricultural Attache in Canberra that 16,480 million hot dogs were produced in America during the previous year, and he had calculated that these would string into 1,820,640 miles of hot dogs which would wrap around the equator seventy-one times. Americans like him could not understand why such thrilling news left Australians cold. The Aussies were so similar to Americans in so many ways that it seemed unnatural for them to prefer hot meat pies to hot dogs. Mr Legge also had news for Australians that one of the biggest American food chains, McDonald's Golden Arches, which sold four million hamburgers a day in the U.S. intended opening for business in Sydney. Australians have a poor opinion of hamburgers along with hot dogs – but Mr Legge was sure that eventually they would come round to the right way of thinking. His main intention was to demonstrate indirectly that the future for exports of Australian meat to the United States was excellent. He revealed that the most consistent user of Australian beef was the Bonanza chain of steak houses which was selling Australian steaks almost exclusively. The owners of the steak houses were 'Hoss' Cartwright and Little Joe of the Bonanza TV series. Australians wondered what was so wrong with all that beef off the Ponderosa if they had to use imported beef.

Most of America's television stars are as well known in Australia as they are in their homeland. American television became as strongly entrenched in Australia from 1956 onwards as had U.S. motion pictures in the 1930s. Applicants for licences for new television stations in Australia solemnly promised the government that they would do their best to use Australian-made shows on their stations as much as was possible. But that was before they discovered the cost of buying a locally produced programme. They found that it was much cheaper to buy programmes from the U.S. or from Britain. An uncritical Australian audience, conditioned to foreign movies, accepted foreign television readily – even when much of it was banal rubbish. An American television show probably cost about $200,000 to produce in the U.S. but after it made its profits above cost in America it could be sold to an Australian television station for as low as $5,000. By contrast an Australian show could be made for as little as $20,000 – or one tenth the cost in the U.S. – but this remained four times the cost of the imported U.S. production which already had paid its way at home.

Even when Australians produced their own television shows many of the top performers in them were Americans. In fact the king of Australian television for many years was a showman from Tennessee, Bob Dyer, who had settled in Australia in the 1930s. Dyer had graduated from vaudeville to Australian radio as a quiz show compere, and from being a radio star he had transferred to television stardom. Australian audiences were saddened by his retirement in 1971. Other expatriate Americans who became top names in Australian television included Don Lane, and Tommy Hanlon Junior. Gerald Stone from Ohio became one of Australia's best known news interviewers. From time to time there were complaints about his American accent from listeners and viewers who thought that he should not involve himself in Australia's current affairs. But Stone became accepted.

The Australian Broadcasting Control Board decided that 50 per cent of programmes on Australian television would have to be of Australian origin by June 1972 – but thinking Australians still worry that Australian television has become a media-colony of the U.S. and Britain. Often Australians have shown by their enthusiastic reception of an occasional top class local production that they are hungry for their own stars, their own writers, and their own shows. Because of the tyranny of television station finances, however, it is evident that foreign domination of Australian television will continue for as long as the Australian government permits it.

Doctor A. Bordow, of Fort Collins, Colorado, who was doing research at the Australian National University into organizational behaviour told me he had become puzzled about the lack of Australian humour in the Australian entertainment field and in the mass media. American situation comedy and slapstick were commonly accepted in Australia as humour – although the more subtle English humour of understatement and satire also seemed to appeal strongly. Doctor Bordow had detected a uniquely Australian type of humour, a droll and dry Will Rogers technique relating to local conditions – 'It's one of those lazy winds. It doesn't go around you, it goes right through you.' But the Australian sense of humour seemed to Doctor Bordow to be a shy violet which seldom made a formal public appearance.

Doctor Bordow had formed theories as to why Americans arriving in Australia felt instantly that they had discovered a way of life similar to their own at home. There were, of course, cultural and military ties between the two countries and there was a WASP component – White Anglo-Saxon Protestant – prevailing in the Australian community. And added to these were European elements which had gone into forming the American nation – migrants from Ireland and Italy and Germany and from Holland, Greece and Spain. But there was also the fact that the Australians knew so much more about the United States than American visitors had at first realized. Australia was a big open ear tuned in to the American news services. In addition the Australians had learned to identify with the American experience as relayed to them through their newspapers, television or cinema. They accepted the U.S. experience and used it as a model.

Figures from the Department of Immigration in Canberra at the beginning of 1972 revealed that more than 78,800 people from the U.S. migrated to Australia for permanent or long-term residence in the post-war years. First inquiries about the possibility of migration to Australia in late 1971 were then running at the rate of about 14,000 a month and they increased in 1972. The loss-rate of American migrants who returned home after trying life in Australia has been high, but more Americans are always in the pipeline ready to give it a go. It has also been right in the historic tradition of a free population flow between the two countries that a lot of Australians have gone to live in the United States. Unfortunately these have included highly-trained people that a country like Australia cannot afford to lose. Higher salaries and greater career challenge in the United States attract such people.

Two enterprising American businessmen, Nick Coburn and Jim Tanner, began a scheme in January 1972 to help prospective American immigrants to decide if they really did wish to settle in Australia before they made the transfer. The scheme, called Sight and Settle, was given the enthusiastic backing of the American Chamber of Commerce in Sydney. It provided chartered aircraft to take Americans to Australia in groups of fifty twice a month to have a fifteen-day tour of the country and to enable them to make a realistic on-the-spot assessment of Australian conditions, both good and bad. Gordon Hooper of California who ran a Sydney-based service, American-Australian Executive Placement Pty Limited, organized seminars for the prospective immigrants.

Hooper said, 'Most of the Americans interested in migrating aren't looking for a better job. It's more an idealistic thing – they want a better country to raise their kids in.'

Loneliness has been blamed for some Americans wanting to hurry home almost as soon as they arrive in Australia. It is the most common and dismaying emotion experienced by all migrants during their first few weeks in a new country. One person who learned about this was Mrs Mary Suplee from Coral Gables, Miami, who arrived in Brisbane in 1965 with her husband, DeWitt. She felt so lonely at first that she could not forget it later after she had become happily settled in Australia. Being a practical and kindly woman Mrs Suplee formed an organization to help other migrants to settle more easily into their new Australian homes and to find new friends and to become part of the Australian scene. She called her organization 'Welcome Waggon of Australia'. Welcome Waggon rapidly became nation-wide. Members of W.W. visited people in their homes, published a newsletter each month and distributed booklets containing information about schools, health schemes, art galleries, bus timetables, and hints on economical meals. Mrs Suplee formed a Newcomers Club in Brisbane for women to enable them to meet regularly at social functions. She also established a co-operative baby-sitting service. One day Mrs Suplee realized that her Welcome Waggon organization was helping more Australians than American migrants. She came to understand that a lot of Australians moving their homes from one Australian State to another or from one city to another were virtually migrants too and became as lonely some times as those from overseas. They were made welcome at Welcome Waggon.

Unlike most settlers from southern Europe and a large proportion of those from Britain most American migrants in Australia are highly educated. Many of them have superior business experience or professional skills which make them well qualified to compete successfully under Australian conditions. Among them have been many school teachers from the 10,000 unemployed school teachers in California in 1971 who found work teaching Australian children. Quite often American migrants also have substantial capital to make a solid start in their new life. Those who do not have much money when they arrive soon seem to acquire it through their American-bred adaptability and competitiveness.

Few Americans have shown more originality in Australia than Don Ewers, a former U.S. marine and a graduate in business administration who had worked in America's guided missile programme. Ewers, aged 47, left Los Angeles in 1955, and bought a small farm at Diamond Creek near Melbourne to raise chickens. In his spare time he went fishing but became irked when he could not buy worms for bait in local stores. In January 1968 Ewers made the momentous decision to breed his own worms. Within two years he was earning $900 a week breeding and marketing 150,000 red wriggler worms every week instead of raising chickens. His greatest breakthrough in business came when he gained a contract to supply live worms to the platypus colony of a wild life sanctuary near Melbourne. As everyone surely knows a platypus eats half its own weight in worms every day. Ewers was made.

Mrs Suplee frequently told her audiences at Welcome Waggon meetings that she constantly warned American migrants that Australia was no Utopia. She told them that Americans who wanted to find everything in Australia that they had left behind in the U.S. should have remained home in the States. It was useless coming to Australia unless they expected differences and were prepared to make adjustments. On the other hand there have been many American migrants who have become so fed up with conditions in the U.S. that they have revelled in what they find in Australia – good and bad lumped together, they have accepted Australia. The easier pace of living in Australia has been the recurring attraction mentioned by Americans who have successfully transplanted themselves. And they are usually not the sort of people who could be classed as drop-outs.

Doctor Eric Matthews from Gramercy Park, Manhattan, went to Australia on a Fulbright Scholarship in the 1960s to study Australian beetles. He returned to America later in 1967 but was soon back in Australia again with his family as migrants. He became Curator of Insects at the South Australian Museum of Natural History in Adelaide. Matthews had several explanations for why he had done it. He was another who liked the easier pace in Australia, and he also thought that Australians were people who really did seem to care if another person lived well or was happy or not. Doctor Matthews was struck by the fact that it seemed much easier to get things done in Australia than in Manhattan. Little things like getting a telephone connected, or putting children into school, or hiring a TV were straight-forward assignments without red tape or delays. But then he made this point: 'In a world that is becoming horribly over-crowded and polluted, Australia may be one of the last lands left where things are still in balance.'

The Australian Department of Immigration sometimes is accused by disgruntled American migrants of concealing less favourable aspects of Australia in its propaganda to gain more white settlers. Maybe there is some justification for these complaints as the Department is not eager to spread bad news about its own country, but equally it is true that it is impossible to please everyone. Some migrants who leave Australia crying that they have been misinformed are trying to cover up their failure to adjust to different conditions. The same people are just as likely to start complaining again once they have arrived home again in the United States, being born belly-achers and chronic losers. The Australian government continues to have more happy-ending migrant stories to plant in home-town U.S. newspapers, and they are always stories meant to deliver a pro-Australian message. Such as:

Mrs Tina Bell's father was Governor Daniel Evans of Seattle. She settled down well in Sydney with her family after her husband had been appointed Vice President of the South East Asian operation of International Nickel, based in Sydney. She became the co-proprietor of one of Sydney's most exclusive art galleries – but her main concern was for her children. She had been worried most of all about how her kids would react to the stricter discipline in Australian schools and the school uniforms which Australian children wore. She reported to her father later that there was no sweat – the children actually liked both.

A new by-pass road which caused a business recession in the town of Tucumcari was the reason why Arthur C. Ross uprooted his family and moved to Australia. He decided that it would be easier to start again in Western Australia where there was a business boom than to try again in another part of the U.S. He was right. He got a million dollar contract in Perth to build apartments and commercial buildings. He found the Western Australian boom like the good old days in the States.

The reasons why Americans have been leaving the United States to try again in Australia have been numerous and widely varied. But foremost among them has been a searching for the kind of life they knew 'in the good old days' – a sad nostalgia for another and happier America they had known and which now seemed lost to them. The American migrants want to live in a part of the world where the worst of the problems of urban-failure have not yet become severe. They are refugees from racial strife, from the American crime or drug problems, from foul city air or impossible traffic jams. To them the quality of life has come to mean more than cash in the bank. Other American refugees are convinced that the United States has become 'sick' and has lost its morality and sense of purpose. But it is significant that many of these people retain their U.S. passports in case they should ever change their minds and wish to return to the United States. Often they are ashamed that they have been forced to flee to Australia from problems at home with which they have not been able to cope.

American migrants sometimes declare after a few weeks in Australia that they have found a country in which living is the way it used to be in the United States years ago. Their kids can go to school unescorted and with no fear of being accosted along the way. It is safe for decent folk to walk through most neighbourhood streets at night without being alert for muggers. Complaints about smog in Sydney and Melbourne do not bother them after what they have known in American cities. Yet many Americans have not been able to continue living in Australia for the very reason that it seems to them to be lagging behind the United States. Sure, the environment is excellent. It is possible to find solitude and peace in the nearest bushland where the only sounds are the sighing of the wind in the gum trees or the calling of the birds. One can just as easily drive along to some beautiful stretch of deserted surfing beach and be the only human for miles, the way it has always been in that part of the South Pacific. Or an American migrant can go to the Northern Territory and re-find the old American West of vast distances and prairies and wild life. Or he can settle in a country town in North Queensland where people want to take you down to the local golf club for a beer as soon as you arrive in town.

Even in the busiest Australian cities, life for the American migrant is most likely to seem easy and uneventful after what he has left back home. But there lies the catch. Many Americans find Australia too easy, uneventful, peaceful and friendly. The best ideals of good neighbourliness and individual freedom of the old United States are still alive in Australia but modern Americans have gotten out of the way of having them. In Australia they are liable to be overcome by a suspicion that they have placed themselves into a backwater of life and are missing out somehow. They have been conditioned since childhood to a faster life, to stiffer competition, to much worse tensions, and to grimmer people. And some of these American migrants cannot endure the change to the slower, happier pace.

Nevertheless the Australian Government remains willing to take a chance and will pay an emigrant from the United States most of the cost of his trans-Pacific fare from the West Coast. In 1972 the Australian Government fare-subsidy for U.S. migrants over the age of 19 was $333. Any American migrant under the age of 19 received Australian assistance of $360 to cover the full fare, and the young migrant paid nothing at all. It was for free. It has been found that the adult Americans most likely to migrate to Australia are the pioneer farmer types, or pioneering businessmen with some capital and an idea for making good in Australia. The wage-earning Americans who have decided that they want to leave the United States for the benefit of their children or for other reasons have usually changed their minds about going to Australia after they have compared its wages and taxes and food and housing costs with those in the U.S. They are told that services are cheaper in Australia and that the social and ecological qualities of Australia are superior – but wage-earners everywhere find it too difficult not to measure success in terms of cash in hand and material possessions, and that sort of success equates with happiness. It is the way that they have been raised to think.

Australians also chase a material standard of living, but most of them continue to have a perception of real values in life. They still try to cling to their fathers' casual assumption of equality and independence belonging to everyone, together with the right to freedom of speech – even if they are no longer quite as game to exercise it as they used to be. They demand plenty of leisure time and rising wages without forfeiting full employment and prosperity. Much of the glitter has faded from the Golden Age dangled before the people in the late 1940s. But while the last vestiges of that exhilarating postwar utopianism survive Australians continue to resent the harbingers of a far less leisurely and less pleasant age who are too ambitious, too hard-working and too 'career-orientated' – as some American migrants in Australia remain.

Even before the 1971-2 recession the much vaunted Australian devotion to a forty-hour working week, with time off to enjoy a quality of life unknown in the U.S., was becoming sadly counterfeit. Many of those Australians who hurried away from their jobs at the end of their work shift were not going to the library to better their minds, nor to the golf course to use their sporting muscles, nor to the company of their families, nor to engage in some absorbing hobby or form of art. No sir, they headed straight for another paying job somewhere else in the city to earn additional money. They had taken a part-time job because they wanted a second car, or a bigger house, or a vacation in Fiji or Japan – or perhaps they had drifted so deeply into debt playing the stock exchange or getting married that they needed two jobs to keep out of the Bankruptcy Court. The Australian Bureau of Census and Statistics discovered that most of them were between the ages of 25 and 34 and were professional or technical people or sales workers. They were the moon-lighters who worked secretly at their second jobs by night when their other employers thought that they were at rest. In May 1971 they made up 3.6 per cent of the total Australian labour force. They had become just as shackled to occupational grindstoning as were Americans.

Some who were honest confessed that if they did not have a second job they would have to send their wives out to work. Often they really did have their 'little woman' out working, but were ashamed and hoped to keep it quiet. In Australia in 1969, 17.3 per cent of married women had paying jobs outside their domestic duties, compared with 23.2 per cent in the United States. By November 1971, 19.5 per cent of married women in Australia were in the work force. If it were not for the Australian legion of working wives some Australian families would be living in tents.

In general, however, Americans are still subjected to much greater pressures and influences to make them work harder and longer than are Australians. Americans, be better educated, tend to desire a more sophisticated and costly way of life than do Australians. They are also exposed to a much greater choice of consumer temptations which are thrust at them almost forcibly night and day, and always demanding the earning and the spending of more and more money.

Just before Christmas in 1971 the American Chamber of Commerce in Australia undertook on its own initiative a survey among U.S. business firms in Australia to learn their opinions on the treatment of women in Australia. Just why the Chamber of Commerce wished to stir up trouble before Christmas is difficult to understand but it went ahead with it. Many of the American businessmen questioned said they believed that Australian women were still being suppressed in what was essentially a masculine society. The Managing Director of an American executive employment firm, Mr Gordon Hooper, observed that in Australia education for women was firmly welded to the objective of turning out good wives and mothers. Mr Hooper seemed to think that there was something wrong with that. He added darkly that the elevation or debasement of women was the surest and most correct measure of the civilization of a people or an age.

Doctor Bordow of the Australian National University was one who refused to accept the proposition that all Australian women should leave for the U.S. at once where they would be better treated. Perhaps American women controlled more money than did women in Australia, but Doctor Bordow was convinced that Australian females had as much power over their men as had their American sisters over theirs. The main difference was that American women were generally more articulate and were better able to express themselves in public. But in the homes it was probably a dead heat.

Although Australian women have not yet learned to organize themselves as well as American women they are learning through the mass media. Women's Lib. ideas originating in the U.S. swiftly become popular in Australia. If women burn their bras in Detroit women in Brisbane are apt to do likewise. Australia is wide open to any new branch of women's organized activities from the U.S. It seems that Australian women are often not able to get enough publicity for their own ideas, and that those who seek to express themselves in public are often thwarted. The so-called women's magazines of Australia are full of the traditional household-hint type of articles and romantic features. Few give any real scope to original female intellect. Outspoken Australian women, therefore, who are not content with tongue-lashing their husbands, friends or neighbours, are driven to making desperation speeches to their own kind at women's clubs or to haranguing the city on radio talk-back programmes. The ideas and the minds of too many intelligent women in Australia are wasted at home or are not developed.

American women are no better off than are those in Australia in many respects not immediately obvious. For instance, they do not have equal pay with men any more than do Australian women. The truth is that discrimination against women in Australia is usually blandly honest and open, whereas in the United States it is often hidden by a male conspiracy. When American women in the United States discover masculine dishonesty, disclosure by disclosure, fuel is fed into the furnace of Women's Lib. and keeps it fiercely hot. Australian women are fully aware right along what the situation is and frequently get square on their menfolk privately and in ways too numerous or subtle to detail.

The ideas and activities of America's various minorities reach Australia. Late in 1971 the American Black Panther movement began influencing Australia's Aborigines. Generally the Australian Aborigines identify more closely with the American Red Indians whose social problems are similar, but some of the Aboriginal leaders adopted the Black Panther movement because they thought it was glamorous and would attract more attention to their claims. During 1972 they began working on finding a fully Aboriginal name and symbol.

More Australian business companies could be following the example of Comalco-Kaiser in doing more to help the Aboriginal communities in the districts in which they are working. Comalco was faced some years ago with the problem of settling, educating and employing the primitive and semi-nomadic tribe which had been roaming and camping on the bauxite deposits of Cape York Peninsula for thousands of years. As Comalco planned to remain in the neighbourhood for about eighty years working the bauxite it was anxious to ensure that the local Aboriginal children received an education to make them employable when they grew up.

The company got the children into school, but the results were disappointing. Those who were not impaired mentally through dietary deficiencies during their infancy or during their mothers' pregnancy still had difficulty in understanding what their teacher was talking about. Comalco tried to see that the children were better fed than ever before, but the language problem was more difficult. When, for example, a teacher asked the children to add up two red pencils and one blue pencil the answer was apt to be a deep and puzzled silence. It was discovered eventually that the kids simply baulked at the words blue and red – as they did at many other words not relating to their austere existence and not in the vocabulary of their parents.

Comalco therefore contributed to an educational research programme launched by the Commonwealth Office of Aboriginal Affairs – a language enrichment course to get pre-school children into shape to understand teachers. It was essentially a long-range experiment conducted in the western New South Wales town of Bourke but the success of it could have wide repercussions.

Any such practical approach to the needs of the Aborigines – even in only one locality – is an improvement on the long-standing Australian practice of callous indifference and neglect and humbug. Some of the foremost hypocrites have been Australian church men, worrying about the distant refugees in India or about infant mortality among the Eskimos, and maybe praying for the Australian Aborigines one Sunday every year but forgetting about them for the rest of the year. Perhaps some American Church might include Australia one day in its active missionary field, and help the Aborigines.

People who become dangerously over-confident, or unaware, in isolation from the competition of the outside world are likely to get hurt when the world catches up with them. This happened to the Aborigines and it has been happening to many of their successors, the modern white residents of Australia.

Too many modern Australians became content with the way things were in their country, and wanted nothing to change nor expected it to. Their priority of thought seldom went beyond the next sporting fixture or the programme for another evening's vacuous intake of American or English television guff. Too many Australians were under-educated but did not care nor thought it mattered nor thought it necessary to keep their children at school. A lot are still under-trained for employment, while others think that a hard day's work is never worth it. Such people cannot reasonably hope to hold onto the high standard of living that they have had the phenomenal good luck to have been enjoying. Some of them have already lost that high standard of living. New vigour and new ideas and new standards imported by newcomers such as the Americans have over-run them.

As Henry Kaiser had remarked someone had to do something about the Australian continent. It could not have remained for ever the world's largest South Sea island where most of the inhabitants sat around in town all day, doing as little as possible and expecting to get away with it indefinitely. Thus it happens that the Americans have been busily settling another frontier with their know-how and their bustling get-up-and-go, aided by their cheque books and the ownership of Australia has been steadily changing hands. The only remaining uncertainty soon will be how much of Australia the Americans will leave to British and Japanese purchasers.

It is not a situation to please the Australian nationalists who see themselves and their fellow countrymen in danger of becoming the hewers of wood and the drawers of water – the labourers for U.S. managers and U.S. stockholders, or the victims of international octupus corporations. Ultimately the solution will lie with the Australian people themselves. They have always believed in their own country's inevitable greatness but now they will have to match that greatness or go under. The Australian people have been caught unprepared, but like it or not they have entered a period of painful national readjustments. Believing in greatness will not be enough to help them.

Australia will continue to be an agricultural nation, a massive producer and supplier of food to the world's markets, and in particular to South East Asia. The nation also must become one of the world's greatest producers of steel, and with all the subsidiary industries allied to steel-making. It would seem incredible and absurd if the Australian government and international money continued to permit the exporting of all the required ingredients for steel-making to distant parts of the world in preference to steel production in Australia, close to sources of raw materials.

But the worsening shortage of fuel and minerals in over-industrialized countries could mean that priority will be given to keeping those nations supplied with Australian materials. In theory any country rich in fuels and other raw materials should be able to dictate terms of supply to nations less fortunate. However, Australia has lost the ownership of a large amount of its birthright and instead of growing strong and wealthy is in danger of being used to keep nations such as the United States and Japan in affluence.

Both the U.S. and Japan have been buying control of fuel and mineral reserves around the world wherever smaller nations have been stupid enough to let them get away with it. This has enabled them to keep prices down while they recklessly continue to increase their industrial growth rates and set targets of over-production.

The United States has extravagantly wasted its own

once enormous natural resources and is moving into a new phase in which its industries will become parasitical, sucking up the reserves of other countries until those too are depleted. Consequently the U.S. government is turning away from philanthropic foreign-aid and will become increasingly imperialistic. Unless strongly resisted the U.S. will be less interested in developing industrial strength in Australia than in channelling Australian resources into the United States where they will help Americans to live a while longer in the magnificent style to which they have become accustomed. In the shorter term Japan will be an even greater danger.

The American experience has demonstrated what can quickly happen, particularly in fuel exhaustion, if resources are not well managed. Not long ago the U.S. had an over-abundance of petroleum but now its industries are turning back to coal and are studying coal-gasification. By 1980 American oil *imports* are expected to rise to 14 million barrels a day to make up the local shortage. Australian oil, liquified natural gas, uranium and coal could vanish even faster if shipped out to gluttonous users. And the present level of foreign ownership could even block Australia from getting a fair price from resources taken.

If Australia is going to be made into a strong and well-balanced nation there needs to be strong government quickly. It will have to undertake extensive economic replanning and a reorganization of Australian industries to supplement and benefit from what has been done by foreign private enterprise and other money. Government in Australia must regain control of its own nation and direct its future or else Australia will remain a political stooge to the United States and will become an economic colony in perpetuity.

Already there is cause for debate as to whether or not an Australian government can regain control. In defence of their ownership of Australian industries American businessmen have spoken glibly of the way that British capital helped to develop the United States – but it took

208

the United States 150 years to free itself of British financial strings. The United States – although the richest nation in the world – did not really break free from British bankers until the Lend-Lease agreements and the financial crippling of Great Britain during the Second World War. The question therefore must be put: how long is it going to take a comparatively weak nation like Australia to throw off foreign-money overlords, whether they be American, British, or Japanese?

It is possible that the Australians have not yet seen the half of it. Money is power wherever it is. Massive foreign-money power can control a nation in ways that Australians have not yet begun to imagine. Without adequate safeguards in Australia there could eventuate private deals between American and Japanese business magnates that could damage the nation's economy. The decisions at board meetings of international corporations could open or shut Australian industries like cupboard doors by granting or denying them their markets or their operating funds. The Australian trade unions could be in for a nasty shock. Extremely wealthy American-owned companies and international corporations are likely to prove formidable opponents in future industrial disputes. They could order large-scale retrenchments or close down their Australian plants or use other forms of retaliation until Australian workers surrendered. There could come a time when the Australian government could find itself under great financial pressure to grant concessions of various kinds to foreign-money overlords or their countries. When a nation has an excess of foreign investment and not enough controls the situation becomes dangerous and the screws are easily turned.

Whether Australians want it or not their nation is now .being reshaped. If they wish to keep up with the changes now being made they will have to change too. They are going to need a sound new national philosophy, and there will have to be a lot of re-thinking. More Australians will have to become dissatisfied with comfortable mediocrity. At some time soon an Australian government is going to have to really start leading the Australian people and the nation instead of just going through the motions like actors in a miming play.

As an Australian, I do not feel optimistic about it. The past record of Canberra's petty-minded selfish politics, expediency, superficial temporary 'solutions', and dodging of responsibilities has been too long-lasting and consistent to engender any confidence in future Canberra administrations. The best administrative brains in Australia are in big business and in the top echelons of the Public Service. Successful businessmen have seldom been attracted into Australian politics. In the Public Service – that excellent administrative machinery designed by the British – brilliant planners too often are bottled up by the political screw top of Parliament.

One day during a luncheon in Canberra the chief of a government department confided in me his conviction that it did not matter too much if he had an unintelligent minister in Parliament – as long as the minister accepted intelligent advice from his department. He added: 'Sometimes it is better to have someone like that at the top.' He was the sort of man who would expect a Sunday driver to get behind the wheel of a Formula One racing car and stay on the track at high speed without crashing. From either viewpoint – from Public Service or Parliament – the Australian system of government has been unsatisfactory. Of course, the past apathy of the people of Australia has deserved and sustained non-government. Australians are becoming aware of this, although not fast enough.

An American suggested to me that the reason for the notorious Australian apathy lies in their centralized system of government. He thought this had made Australians more homogenous than the people of the United States, and that people all over Australia looked to Canberra helplessly and accepted situations which they felt powerless to alter. But then again it is possible that Australians have still not fought their way out of the emasculating, enervating vacuum created by the skilful administrators of the British Colonial Office. Whatever has been the cause of it the people of Australia are going to have to snap out of it fast or rue the consequences.

Many have wondered what would have been the effect upon the Australian character had the United States forces in 1942 not been able to save the country from enemy invasion. Possibly if major land battles had been fought on Australian soil before the Japanese had been thrown back the Australian nation today would be more mature, more dynamic, more united and more self-reliant. Perhaps a searing experience of that kind is needed to harden a nation and teach it what the world is all about.

Bibliography

Norman Bartlett *The Goldseekers*, (Jarrolds, London, 1965)

James Peter Birrell *Walter Burley*, (Queensland University Press, Brisbane, 1965)

Rafaello Carboni *The Eureka Stockade*, (Melbourne University Press, Melbourne, 1963)

E. Daniel & A. Potts (eds.) *A Yankee Merchant in Gold-rush Australia*, (Heinemann, Melbourne, 1970)

H. Hunt (ed.) *George Francis Train, American Merchant*, (G. P. Putnam & Co., New York, 1857)

Charles Hursthouse Jnr *Emigration*, (Robert Hardwicke, London, 1853)

Dudley McCarthy *Official War History S.W. Pacific Area – 1st year*, (Australian War Memorial, Canberra, 1959)

Sir H. G. Raggatt *Mountains of Ore*, (Lansdowne Press, Melbourne, 1968)

Ernest Scott (ed.) *Lord Robert Cecil's Goldfields Diary*, (Melbourne University Press in association with Oxford University Press, Melbourne, 1935)

A. G. L. Shaw *The Economic Development of Australia*, (Longmans of Australia, Melbourne, 1944)

Griffith Taylor *Australia*, (Methuen & Co., London, 1959)

Clive Turnbull *Bonanza, The Story of George Francis Train*, (Hawthorn Press, Melbourne, 1946)

Mark Twain *Following the Equator, a Journey around the world*, (Harper, New York, 1925)

Lionel Gage Wigmore *The Long View, A History of Canberra*, (F. W. Cheshire, Melbourne, 1963)

Eric Williams *From Columbus to Castro. The History of the Caribbean 1942-69*, (Andre Deutsch Ltd, London, 1970)